Network Programming under VMS/DECNet Phases IV and V

Network Programming under VMS/DECNet Phases IV and V

Edward B. Toupin

Trademarks and trademarked material mentioned in this book include Digital Equipment Corporation, DECNet, DNA, DDCMP, NSP, Phase IV, Phase V, NICE, CMIP, MICE, MEN, FAL, DAP, NCP, OSI, TCP/IP, SNA, Ethernet, X25, VMS.

The cover graphic is reprinted with permission of the publisher, from *Issues and Problems in Computer Networking*, © 1990 Bill Hancock. Published by AMACOM, a division of the American Management Association. All rights reserved.

© 1993 QED Publishing Group
P.O. Box 812070
Wellesley, MA 02181-0013

Library of Congress Catalog Number: 92-3416
International Standard Book Number: 0-89435-441-8

93 94 95 10 9 8 7 6 5 4 3 2 1

Library of Congress Cataloging-In-Publication Data
  Toupin, Edward B.
      Network programming under VMS/DECNet phases IV and V /
  Edward B. Toupin.
          p.   cm.
      Includes bibliographical references (p.   ) and index.
      ISBN 0-89435-441-8
      1. VAX computers—Programming.   2. C (Computer program
  language) 3. VAX/VMS.   4. DECnet (Computer network
  architecture) I. Title.
  QA76.8.V32T68   1993
  005.7'1245—dc20   92-3416
                                                        CIP

In memory of Edward Pennison

Contents

List of Illustrations

List of Tables

Preface

There have been many outstanding papers written in the area of network programming as well as documentation to assist in building network applications. The main problem is that none of these papers provide a basic introduction to network programming. The intent of this book is not to review the current documentation but instead to give the reader a firsthand view of how some very interesting communication paradigms are implemented in order to be able to understand other related documents. From here the reader will have a basic understanding of some of the concepts involved in network programming so that additional information will be clearly understood from a general foundation.

The original documents, on which this book is based, were notes taken during the development of a set of provers, that is, sample test applications. The main idea behind the provers was to demonstrate applicable capabilities of the Digital network architecture and the ideas of connectionless and connection-oriented communications. During the initial planning and design stages for the sample applications, a means had to be devised that mixed client/server applications with peer-to-peer operations. The applications operated in a distributed environment where communications for external processing and interfacing was required. The solution to an overall system was to implement a flexible network interfacing application—but what type?

There were several vendor applications available but none provided the flexibility that was required for the implementation. The first phase utilized transparent interprocess communications, which proved to be quite cumbersome for multiple processes. The next step was broadcasting, which forced every receiver on the network to process the respective information in order to properly determine the destination. Step three was to implement multicasting, which was fantastic and provided the flexibility required for the implementation. Once each of these areas was reviewed, a legitimate set of primitives was designed to perform connectionless and connection-oriented applications easily . This book will take the information found at the beginning of the aforementioned research and provide it to the reader to demonstrate how these particular methods work at a lower level.

Once the network processes had been designed, a means of monitoring the network had to be designed to monitor the impact of the new applications on the network. This led to an intelligent network management system that allowed monitoring and control of the network devices from a central node. This implementation took into account network utilization calculations, device control, and busiest-node calculations as well as flash flood control and loopback tests. All of this was implemented with the tools designed from the communication applications except that it was tackled from a different angle. This particular application and set of tools will not be reviewed but this area of research is quite interesting, and it is suggested to the curious reader that the area of network management be investigated to see a different angle for the implementations to be provided.

ORGANIZATION

This book has been written to allow the basic concepts to be presented briefly with working examples. The organization of this book allows each concept to build on top of the previous one to allow the flow of information to be easily understood for both connectionless and connection-oriented applications.

The first chapter is merely an overview of the entire scope of the book and how this book came about. This chapter provides a brief insight into how the information available in this book was assembled and contains directions for the research included within. In order to provide a basis for the remainder of the book, a couple of scenarios are given that will be followed in each of the following chapters.

The second chapter outlines the basic architecture of a network and provides a very brief overview of the Digital Network Hierarchy. This section is not meant to make the reader an expert on network architecture; instead it will provide a foundation for the remainder of the information to be given in the book. The information is given from the author's view and is a conglomeration of several different explanations given to the author. The primary purpose of this chapter is to explain how the network hierarchy operates in a manner that can be easily assimilated for use in the detailed explanations of both connection-oriented and connectionless communications.

The third chapter covers the Ethernet frame formats and the contents thereof. Specifically, the information covers the frame format and how to acquire the information required for the field contents of the frames as well as how to build and manage frames. This chapter will provide an explanation of the padded and nonpadded frames to provide a broad base for uses of the Ethernet frame.

The fourth chapter covers network programming basics including the VMS System Service calls required to perform network communications. This chapter will reduce the plethora of System Service calls to just a few to eliminate some of the confusion in becoming accustomed to network programming. The primary purpose of this chapter is to focus attention on the absolute basics, but it will provide a base understanding of how these functions are used to develop more complex applications later.

Once the basics are covered, the book moves into connection-oriented applications with Transparent Interprocess Communications. The fifth chapter covers the phases of TIPC as well as how to implement the communication method. The end of the chapter covers several different configurations for TIPC to provide some workable views of the method. This chapter is more or less unique in that it is the only one covering information on connection-oriented applications and is very important in that the base information provided will be used for comparisons in the discussions on connectionless implementations.

Chapters Six, Seven, and Eight cover three methods of connectionless communication implementations covering multicasting, broadcasting, and explicit addressing, respectively. The information for each of the three chapters builds until Chapter Eight, where the information is consolidated to provide an overview of a client/server implementation using all three of the connectionless communication paradigms. While the configurations provided are examples and, in some cases, subsets of larger applications, the primary objective of the examples is to provide a common base for explanation. This will allow the user to understand the basics of two or three scenarios and how the implementations can operate and compare in each.

Chapter Nine is a brainstorming chapter and provides the reader with general ideas regarding the information presented in the book. One of the topics involves a discussion of which method, connection or connectionless, is better under which circumstances as well as the pros and cons of both methods. Other brainstorming topics include a general overview of how the methods presented can be used in protocol conversion, an experimental compression protocol, and a brief explanation of how remote procedure calls can be implemented. While reading this chapter, keep in mind that the ideas are not presented in great detail and are only representations of ideas where the code given in the book can be utilized.

Finally, the back matter contains information referenced throughout the text but falls outside of the scope of this book. Appendix A maintains a table of protocols that can, for example, be utilized in multicasting applications. Appendix B depicts code that can be used with service access points and follows the explanation of service access points in Chapter Nine. Appendix C gives sample code that follows with the brief mention of shared protocols in several sections of the book including Chapter Nine. The bibliography contains valuable resources that should be referenced to allow for detailed explanations of primitives required for network programming under VMS with DECNet.

SAMPLE CODE

One prerequisite for reading this material is that the reader must be able to understand the C programming language. All of the material is based on research and prover applications written in the C language in order to provide a semi-common thread to the readers. For each subject discussed, full C examples are given to permit the general concepts and operations to be explained as well as other examples located at the end of the book that are not directly explained in the text. Being a programmer, the author is aware that it is easier to see the code with an explanation than to see an explanation without any examples whatsoever. This was noticed during most of the research for the provers given in this book. These ideas are not meant to represent the end of the network programming realm but are only a small piece and should be used to spark new ideas for future implementations. The paradigms explained were utilized in some general-purpose applications that provide some interesting concepts for other accessible realms.

SUMMARY

This book is not necessarily meant for leisure reading but is instead intended for reference during the development of network-related applications. Do not take this work as the only reference for network programming but instead use it to assist in moving forward into other applications. There is a plethora of information available on network programming; however, it is widely dispersed. Use this book to assist in locating more in-depth information for future network programming development and to provide a foundation of understanding for further research.

Good luck in your endeavors.

Acknowledgments

This book was written with the help of some good folks who were willing to share their ideas and experience in order to provide the information required to accomplish the applications and associated tasks.

Thanks to Bernie Toupin for his assistance in investigating the provers outlined in this book. It was a discussion that we had about a year ago that pushed the research for the provers forward. Bernie's explanation of communication methods assisted considerably in current research directions.

Thanks to Tory Toupin, Phi Beta Kappa, for relating his experience of process communications and management from a UNIX developer's standpoint. The information Tory provided gave a firm foundation of generic communication scenarios as well as remote procedure calls and the TCP/IP standards. Good luck on the Osiris Project.

Finally, but most importantly, thanks to Digital Equipment Corporation for the consistent effort put into the development and maintenance of their products. Great job! Also, thanks to all of those at Digital who answered my multitude of questions and helped me move forward with this project.

The author would like to hear from any readers who may have comments, suggestions or related information. Please forward all messages to INET:toupine@casi.cba.du.edu, PRODIGY : RBFD19A or P.O. Box 44231, Denver, CO 80201.

Introduction

During the development of several network-oriented applications, a means of utilizing the distributed nature of the Digital
architecture had to be devised. One of the main problems involved with this development was that of the lack of consolidated
information. It took several months to find the information required for DECNet programming, then another month to assimi-
late the data. Once the information was eventually put into an
orderly format, it was found that a lot of implementations utilizing low-level network programming were not directly available
for research-related use. A majority of the references pointed to-
ward vendor software; however, this direction would not allow
the flexibility required. In order to provide the flexibility and
distributed nature required, a custom interprocess communication reference library was designed and implemented for current
and future developments.

The original premise of this book was to provide a general
view of information available for DECNet Phase IV/V programming. After reviewing the research material on which this book
is based, as well as the abundant Digital and third-party manu-
als, the number of volumes required to cover the entire realm of
network programming would rival the Oxford English Dictionary. Another point was brought into consideration: if this book

were to cover general topics in network-oriented programming, it would simply be a repeat of the documentation already available. Based on these facts, the revised premise is to provide a "how to" book. The reader will be provided with a brief overview of networks as a whole followed by actual implementations and associated code. Once the base implementations and code have been presented, the reader can easily move forward to build on top of the topics presented with the code provided.

This book has been written about low-level DECNet Phase IV/V programming on VAX/VMS using the VAX C programming language. One of the main purposes of this book is to consolidate the plethora of information available on DECNet programming into one easy-to-read and easily accessible volume. As the reader delves into the ideas presented in this book, he or she must understand that low-level network programming is not as straightforward as developing concurrent applications on a single host. Network programming itself is a task combining synchronization, contention, and related imaginable horrors. Now imagine synchronization mixed with multiprocess communications across a network as well as low-level network interfacing. Combining the idea of concurrent programming with network programming adds a whole new dimension to the word programming and is otherwise known as distributed application development.

The original documents in this book are a series of notes taken during the development of a set of provers, that is, sample test applications. The main idea behind the provers was to discover how to implement different communication paradigms without having to rely on vendor-related interfacing applications. As previously stated, it was difficult to find information specifically on multicasting, broadcasting, explicit addressing, and related interprocess communications to provide a foundation for development. This situation made the provers and associated notes the only consolidated references available for the required work.

For each subject discussed, full examples are given to permit the general concepts and operations to be explained as well as a series of other examples located at the end of the book that are not directly explained in the text. Being a programmer, the author is aware that it is easier to see the code with an explanation than to see an explanation without any examples whatsoever.

These ideas are not meant to represent the end of the network programming realm but instead are to spark new ideas in the reader's mind for further implementations. Example paradigms are given explaining how each implementation may fit into the respective paradigms in order to open new doors for the reader. Some of the paradigms explained were utilized in some sample applications and others were related to full-scale working applications developed by the author that provide some interesting concepts for other accessible realms.

To provide additional topics for the reader, a section has been included in order to provide information on future research in the areas of protocol conversion and the development of a compression protocol for an experimental communications application. Protocol conversion is currently in use by many vendors and can be found in host-based gateways as well as, for example, UNIX (TCP/IP) to VMS (DECNet) communications subsystems. When discussing a compression protocol, this idea (as far as this book is concerned) is still on the drawing board; however, the information provided here would allow the reader to understand the concepts behind customized protocol implementations for further development.

SAMPLE IMPLEMENTATIONS

Before delving into specifics, let's look at a few paradigms in order to provide a base for all future explanations. For this instance, assume that a method of data transfer is required in a general-purpose environment. If the processes are on the same machine and a lot of data is required rapidly, then of course the processes can use a shared image or a global section can be implemented. If the data exchange for the two local processes is minimal, a logical definition or a disk-based file can be used. What if the processes are on different machines? Well, the processes can simply read and write from a file on one of the machines, but that would saturate the network and it would be incredibly slow. What if the remote processes need speed with minimal network usage and the system administrator does not appreciate a fragmented disk from constantly accessing the disk-based file? Interprocess communications is the answer!

Taking the idea of allowing two processes to communicate

over a network, let's take a look at a couple of sample paradigms in order to allow for a basis of understanding for the direction of this book. The information provided here is not everything about network programming, but is designed to provide a foundation of information to the reader to get started in the area of workable and expanding network applications.

A Health Check Scenario

A health check scenario provides a means of verifying a system's integrity. Assume, as in Figure 1.1, that there exists a process, ProcessA, on Node01 and a second process, ProcessB, on Node02. The two processes are identical in operation; however, one process, ProcessB, is dormant while the other process, ProcessA, is active. The health check scenario comes into effect where the two respective processes need to know the state of each other for proper system-wide operation.

A primary process, ProcessA, maintains a communications link to a second process, ProcessB. ProcessA occasionally checks the respective health of ProcessB in order to know how to handle certain processing situations based on the respective state. Let's look at a distributed database application where the database itself maintains a list of people's names and addresses. Under normal operations, users request and update the information da-

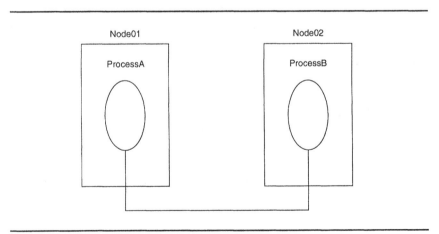

Figure 1.1.   A two-process health check scenario.

tabase via ProcessA, the primary process. If ProcessA should drop out at any time, ProcessB will notice that ProcessA is down by means of the respective health check. At this point, ProcessB will maintain all user requests until a positive health check message is transferred from ProcessA to ProcessB.

As can be seen in Figure 1.2, the primary purpose of such an implementation is to provide a backup process in case the primary process is no longer active. Assume that the name and address

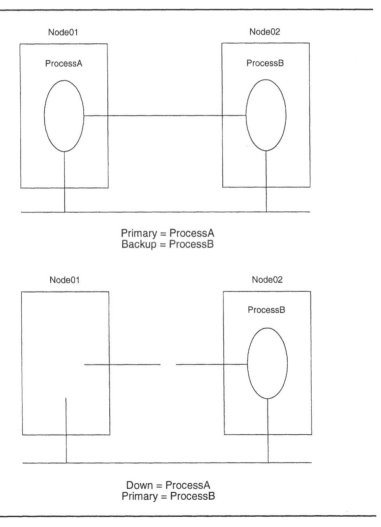

Figure 1.2. States of primary and backup processes.

database exists in an insurance office where access to client information is imperative. In such a situation, a backup database process is always required in case ProcessA should cease operating for any reason. Likewise, ProcessB can be dropped at any time in order to perform maintenance while ProcessA maintains operation. The health check provides a means of knowing which process is to perform operations on user requests while providing a backup for all information management. The data is transparently available to all users regardless of the state of the backup and primary processes.

A Client/Server Scenario

A client/server scenario provides a means of allowing multiple users access to a centralized data server in a transparent fashion. This situation will lend itself to the previous example of a name and address database where users may retrieve and update information as required.

As depicted in Figure 1.3, the client processes communicate with a server process in order to transfer requests and data between the respective processes. During a request from a client process to retrieve a record from the server process's name and

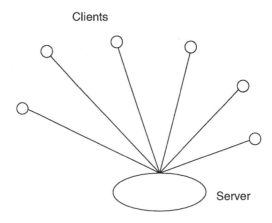

Figure 1.3.   Client/Server.

address database, the request is packaged and sent to the server process. The server process receives the request, processes the information, then transfers the response back to the requesting client process. Likewise, a client process may send a request to modify a database record while, for instance, another client process is viewing that same database record. Once the update has been sent to the server process to modify the respective record, the information is repackaged and sent out by the server process to the viewing client process in order to keep all client processes up to date.

ONWARD

The primary point to be made here is that no matter which of these situations is reviewed, the common function required for proper operation is that of some type of interprocess communications. This is the area that will be covered in this book in order to provide the reader with a basis for further network-oriented applications. Once this basis is established, full applications may be developed that are built on the basic ideas provided. Throughout the remaining chapters, keep these two examples in mind for reference purposes to allow a basic foundation for explanation that will provide a better understanding of the concepts in this book.

Networks

This section will provide the reader with a brief overview of the Digital Network Architecture and related network functions. The premise of this section is not to make the reader an expert on network operation and topologies, but will instead give the reader general knowledge of networks for in-depth explanations into the operations and implementations of some very important network programming strategies. The information provided simply skims the surface; however, this information is the basis for the examples given in each chapter discussing direct network access.

NETWORK DEFINITION

For all practical purposes, a network consists of at least two or more nodes that communicate over a common physical link (see Figure 2.1). Nodes on a DECNet network operate as equals, or peers, where no one system has control over another. For networking, this means that any node on a network can communicate with any other node on the network. The main advantage to this type of operation is that one node may be responsive to another without intervention by a third. Through this direct type of access, communication overhead is decreased and overall net-

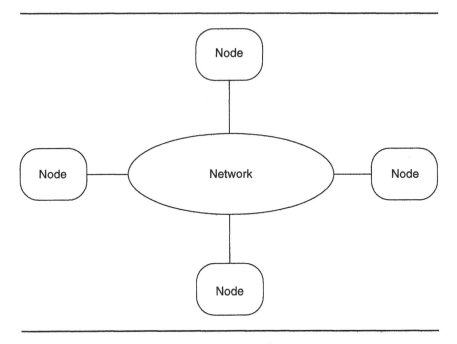

Figure 2.1.   Depiction of a network configuration.

work performance increases as opposed to the network performance in a network maintained using intervening nodes. By the
same token, vendor-specific applications can be introduced to the
DECNet hierarchy that may easily interface to the network by
means of vendor-specific protocol implementations.

All systems that are connected to the network communicate as
peers, which means that all nodes have an equal share of network
resources and do not communicate through a central server, or
host. Because of this configuration, any node on the network can
communicate with any other node on the network, and not only to
those that are immediately connected to that node. Also allowed
by this configuration is program facility sharing by way of allowing the user to log-on to a remote node and access the available
resources of the respective node. DECNet networks link comput-
ers in a configuration that provides the ability to share resources,
exchange information, and implement the idea of distributed processing. The idea behind distributed processing involves the place-
ment of systems where they are needed instead of moving the

respective area to the system. From each of these remote systems, information may be originated and distributed to other nodes in the network. Information is available wherever it is needed and may be distributed to all parts as required. An entire network may allow access to any unit, at any time, for any related purpose, by any node.

NETWORK OPERATION

The idea behind information transfer over the network involves the movement of data from a source system to a destination system. Each system is known as a *node,* which is logically connected over a *circuit* to another node. The circuit, being a logical connection, is routed through a *line,* or physical connection. The line itself is the communication path that connects all nodes to the network and may be any device or combination of devices including coaxial cable, modems, and so forth. A circuit is a higher-level path between nodes that uses the line to carry the information between the respective nodes. See Figure 2.2.

At a higher level, a *logical link* connects processes on separate machines, or on the same machine, for communication purposes. Each of these logical links allows the respective process to transfer the desired data across the circuits to the process on the destination machine. The respective processes mentioned are known as *network objects.* See Figure 2.3.

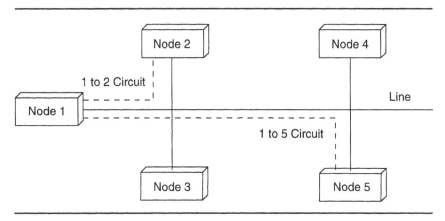

Figure 2.2.   Circuit and line connections in a network.

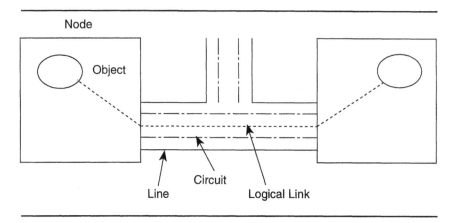

Figure 2.3.   Discrete components of a logical link.

NETWORK ADDRESSING

Since all nodes are connected to a single physical link, a means of determining which node is to receive a respective frame[1] has been devised that utilizes individual node addresses. Each node is assigned a 48-bit (6-byte) address that is unique to each particular machine and is assigned to the controller, for all practical purposes, at startup. Once the machine has registered its address with its controller, it will intercept any frame that maintains a destination address equal to that of the respective node. In order to direct a frame to the node, each frame contains a destination address and control information as well as the data to be transmitted to the destination node. In its simplest form, the control information consists of a source address, destination address, protocol value, and data.

The address of the node, as previously stated, contains 6 bytes, usually containing the hex value of AA as the first byte. At this point, do not confuse the hardware address of a node with the software address. The hardware address is assigned to the controller by the device's vendor, while the software address may be assigned by the system administrator at the time of installation. The way to denote a hardware address is by a hex value of 08 or 09 in the first byte of the respective address. The final two

---

[1]A frame is an entity transferred onto the network.

bytes of the software address denote the unique node address. These two bytes are utilized by the respective DECNet control layers to locate the node name based on the address in the network database as well as to determine if the frame is destined for that node.

The frames on the network may be exchanged between nodes on the network even if the nodes are not directly connected (i.e., the same line). In order for this type of communication to occur, an intervening node is required in order to properly assign the frame down the correct path to the destination node. One type of these intervening nodes is known as *routers* as opposed to the standard receiving nodes, known as *end nodes*. The difference between the end nodes and the routers is that routers have multiple circuits and may forward frames on behalf of another node, while end nodes may not forward frames and may have only one active circuit at any given time. See Figure 2.4.

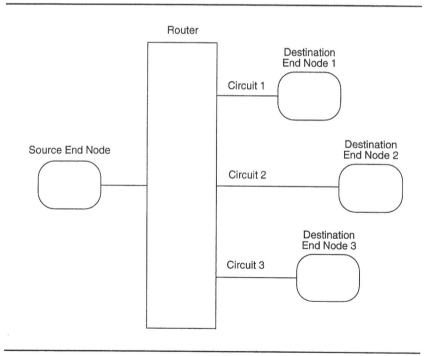

Figure 2.4.   Routing from a source node to one of three destination nodes.

In order to route messages, a router maintains a database of available paths to destination nodes. This information is kept up to date by exchanging *hello* messages with adjoining devices in order to determine *what* is connected to the respective router's circuits. When the router receives a frame destined for a node on one of the router's outgoing channels, the router uses the database information to determine the most efficient, or least costly, path to the destination node and forwards that frame down the respective circuit to that node.

DECNET HIERARCHY

The Digital Network Architecture (DNA) is the basis for all Digital network communications. As can be seen in Figure 2.5, DNA Phase IV and V contain several different layers that provide different levels of interaction between nodes on a network. DNA is arranged in a hierarchical set of layers, each of which maintains its own level of functionality for network operations as a whole. The main purpose of this hierarchy is to provide flexibility to allow the incorporation of user- or vendor-supplied network communication technologies as well as advanced protocol-oriented communications between individual layers of the hierarchy. This section will provide a brief overview and comparison of the different layers of Phase IV and V. With respect to the applications in this book, all explanations will be generic to avoid limiting the applications to one specific DECNet implementation. Note that DEC has designed the Phase V implementation to be capable of supporting equipment and software conforming to Phase IV networking standards.

Layer 8

Phase IV. Layer 8 of DNA is known as the user layer and can be thought of as the user interface for the DNA. This is the first layer that interacts with a user application and involves all user-oriented programs and services that access the network and related system entities. At this top level, users and user processes alike have access to the sharing of resources, communications, remote file access across the network, and file transfers between nodes as well as related database management capabilities. One additional interfacing process in the user layer is the Network Control Program (NCP), which allows users access to lower modules of the DNA hierarchy for network-oriented control functions.

Phase V. In Phase V, this layer is not explicitly defined; however, it is referenced as an application processing layer in which all related processes interact with the DNA.

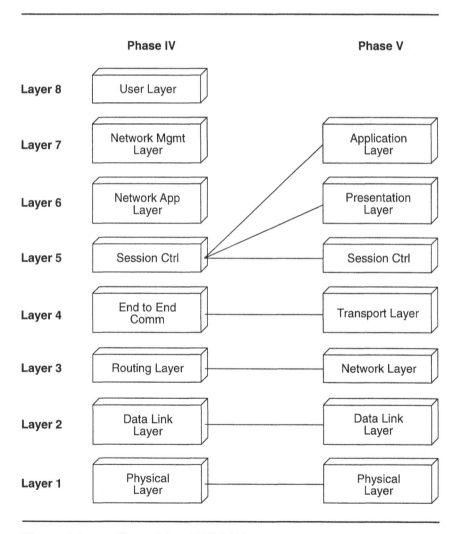

Figure 2.5.   Phase IV and V DECNet layers.

Layer 7

Phase IV. The network management layer allows all user layer processes access to the network functions for interaction with the network in such a way as to transparently perform network-oriented actions. The layer maintains available functions for network management as well as direct access to all layers immediately below in order to modify the respective node's characteristics with the network. This module utilizes the Network Information and Control Exchange (NICE) protocol for network-related management functions. Refer to the *DECNet Digital Architecture Phase IV Network Management Functional Specification* for more information on the NICE protocol.

Phase V. There is no direct correlation between Phase IV and V for layer 7. In this instance, network management functions are not accessible by one single layer but are managed through interfaces to a network management component by each architectural layer. Under Phase V, the primary protocol is the Common Management Information Protocol (CMIP), which is composed of the Management Information Control and Exchange (MICE) and Management Event Notification (MEN) protocols.

In Phase V, layer 7 equates to the application layer. This layer is concerned with functions that allow user applications to use the network for communications as well as allow communications with lower layers of the DNA. This layer is very flexible in its interface because of the wide variety of applications that will require access to the lower layers. This layer is, in essence, the interface for the OSI layers to allow access to system-wide network functions by user applications.

Layer 6

Phase IV. The network application layer is an extension of the network management layer and user layer in that it contains functions that are required by these respective layers. In this layer, for one example, remote file access is accomplished by means of the local layer and the remote file access listener (FAL), located in the network application layer on the remote node. In this instance, the layer receives a request from the previous layer that corresponds to a file-related action to be taken on a remote node. The layer and the file access listener on the remote node communicate over an established logical link using the data access protocol (DAP). All related functions accessible in the previous two layers are maintained and controlled from this layer and include functions such as remote file management, remote terminal access, and related functions.

Phase V. The presentation layer is concerned with how multiple entities communicate with each other. In this instance, one entity may communicate with another without being concerned about the syntax of that communication. In one instance, the presentation layer is responsible for establishing a common *language* between the communicating entities. In another instance, where the entities are not communicating with a common language, the presentation layer will convert the transferred syntax between the entities to accommodate the difference.

Layer 5

Phase IV. The session control layer is the central module for interprocess communications between processes on separate nodes or on a local node. As related to user applications, this layer matches all logical links submitted by layer 4 between local and remote user processes. Associated with link management, modules in this layer monitor and maintain access control capabilities from remote links and related access requests. Regarding name management for the network, this layer performs all network database information management in order to allow name-to-address translation for proper node address assignment for frame transmission. The Phase IV implementation currently performs operations that are now implemented in the application, presentation, and session control layers for Phase V.

Phase V. In a manner similar to the Phase IV implementation, the Phase V session control layer provides a means of organizing information transfer between entities as well as retrieving and managing object attribute information. This layer also performs address resolution by accessing the naming service to determine the given name of object, protocol, and addressing information for local or remote object access. Once an object's identity is established, the session control layer of Phase V performs link establishment by way of the transport layer.

Layer 4

Phase IV/V. The end-to-end communications layer of Phase IV is similar to the Phase V transport layer. This layer maintains the transport for node-to-node communications over the network as well as maintain a dependable data transfer mechanism between users (i.e., user processes). The functions maintained in this module include the management of logical links between processes/objects, information flow, and transmission error control management. Another area covered by this layer is that of the reassembly of dissected messages. One example is that of transferring a large message from Node01 to Node02. In such a situation, the message must be broken into separate parts in order to be managed properly by the network. This layer will receive the disassembled message and reassemble the data for the session control layer on the receiving end of the respective link. This layer also performs disassembly of the respective information for transmission of a large message to the respective node at the opposite end of the link. Protocols maintained in this layer are the Class 0, 2, and 4 OSI protocols in Phase V as well as the DEC Transport protocol, Network Services Protocol (NSP), in Phase IV and V.

Layer 3

Phase IV/V. The routing layer of Phase IV is similar to the network layer of Phase V. This layer provides a means of transferring packets[2] over the appropriate path in order to reach the destination node specified in the destination address of the respective packet. For instance, if there should exist several paths available from the respective node, this layer determines the best path to transmit the packet in order to reach the respective

---

[2]A packet is an entity transferred between layers 2 and 3.

destination node. This type of situation is not specific to DECNet-related protocols but also applies to the fact that other such protocols and/or paths may be available for the node. This means that the respective path is chosen by this layer to route the packet through the data link layer module associated with that path and/or protocol.

Layer 2

Phase IV/V. The data link layers in Phase IV and V are identical in that they are both concerned with communications between the upper layers of the DNA and the physical layer. The data link layer defines the means of communication between nodes regardless of the respective vendor or user protocol. This layer acts as a translator for the respective node in order to eliminate any concern about the type of transport utilized between the communicating nodes. Another responsibility of this layer is that of maintaining error-free transmission and reception on the line connecting the nodes on the network. An example of data link modules would be a node configuration that maintains several protocols. Each respective protocol module connects to layer 3 and registers itself as a particular protocol handler (i.e., 0x0660 for user applications). During transmission of a packet destined for a user application, layer 3 would send that packet to the layer's module registered with the user protocol. The same applies to packet reception where the data link module registered as a user protocol would receive all user-destined packets.

Layer 1

Phase IV/V. The physical layers in Phase IV and V are identical in that they are both concerned with the transmission of information on the available network medium. The physical layer maintains the device drivers, controllers, and related devices that attach a node to the network. This layer defines how the device drivers and hardware should transmit data over any available transmission lines. This layer also maintains modules for monitoring channels for traffic and collisions, and for the synchronization of the layer based on the preamble transmission and during transfer as well as a module for informing the data link layer when a transmission has been completed.

PROTOCOL DEFINITION

In order to reduce the amount of processing involved at each node, protocols are utilized that allow direct communication between similar modules located on separate nodes. This type of communication allows direct communication between the respective modules for module-related management messages. A protocol is a means of handling certain frames based on the frame's type or protocol identifier. Users and vendors alike may provide their own protocols so long as these protocols are consistent across the network between source and destination objects. For example, a user application registered as protocol 0x0660 on Node01 communicates with a secondary process on Node02 registered as the same protocol. In such a situation, all related frames are routed directly between the respective processes based on protocol 0x0660 for protocol-specific processing.

COMMUNICATION CAPABILITIES

From a programmer's standpoint, there are a few very important means of transferring data between processes, or objects, on different nodes. Each method has its advantages and disadvantages; however, each provides a great deal of flexibility in the DECNet hierarchy. Four of the primary methods that are to be discussed in this book include Transparent Interprocess Communications, Multicasting, Broadcasting, and Explicit Addressing.

Transparent Interprocess Communications

TIPC allows processes to communicate with each other over a logical link established by calls to functions within layer 4 in the respective nodes of the communicating processes. The function call includes addressing information of the target process (i.e., process and node) located on the remote node. The calls are independent of the respective operating system and programming language that provides for a common foundation for system communication and integration. The only concern is that the respective protocol management facilities are consistent between the processes.

Once the logical link is established, either process may send or receive data over that logical link. To send data over the link, a source process issues a request for transmission, while the receive process sends a request to receive said transmission. In this instance, layer 4 of the sender transfers this data over a logical link to layer 4 of the receive node. The receive process is then passed the respective data for appropriate processing.

Multicasting Communications

MCAST is a means of communicating with one or more nodes simultaneously without creating a direct logical link. Multicasting essentially eliminates any specific logical links between processes on different machines and instead allows the information to travel within the local network to all nodes. This method bypasses several layers within the DECNet hierarchy and actually allows the user process control over communication for that process below layer 4. It is the responsibility of the receiving nodes to determine whether the respective node should accept the frame. All nodes that maintain multicasting capabilities will capture the frame; however, only those nodes with the respective destination multicast address will pass the frame to the vendor/user application for processing.

Broadcasting Communications

BCAST is implemented when a frame is submitted to the network that is accepted and processed by all nodes on the network. Broadcasting is similar to multicasting in some respects; however, the programmer has much less control over the destinations since all registered nodes receive and process that frame. As with multicasting, this method bypasses the higher layers of DNA to control the network functions at a lower level.

Explicit Addressing

EADRS is similar to transparent interprocess communications except for the fact that a direct logical link is not established and the process controls the network interface at a lower layer. In its simplest form, from a programmer's point of view, the frame is simply submitted to the network and captured by whichever machine matches the destination address within the frame. EADRS emulates TIPC but at a lower level. Recall that in TIPC, a link is requested through layer 4 to an explicit remote node object. All information is transferred over that link to that remote object. In EADRS, no explicit link is established but instead a destination address is built by the transmitting user process and given to the frame. The frame is then placed onto the network and picked up by the remote node specified as the destination. This situation brings into play protocol-related implementations for frame management between nodes/objects on the network.

SAMPLE COMMUNICATION FLOW

The primary purpose of a network is to transfer information from a source node to a destination node. Each piece of data that is passed across the network starts at a user process, then travels down through the DNA hierarchy and out the physical layer. If the respective destination node is not on the local network, it travels up to layer 3 of an adjacent routing node where it is sent out the next line. The frame is eventually intercepted by the destination node and travels up the respective DNA hierarchy until it reaches the destination process. The following sections detail the flow of a message from the user process to a destination process, including each level of the DNA hierarchy and related network architecture. See Figure 2.6.

Source Node

A user process, PROCA, at NODE01 requires the transmission of some data to a process, PROCB, on NODE02. PROCA immediately submits a connection request to NODE02::PROCB by passing the respective node and object connection information to layer 5. At this point, the layer uses the node name NODE02 to locate the numeric address of NODE02 in the network data-

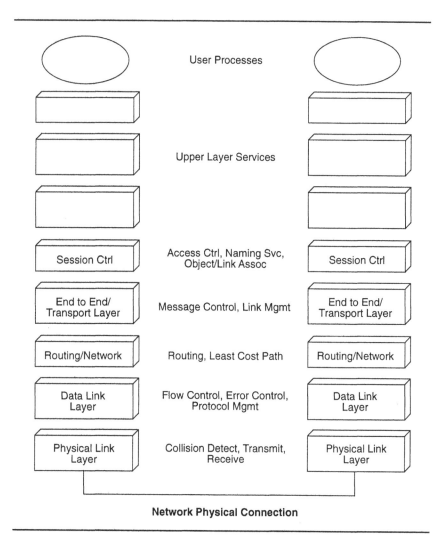

User Processes

Upper Layer Services

Session Ctrl	Access Ctrl, Naming Svc, Object/Link Assoc	Session Ctrl
End to End/ Transport Layer	Message Control, Link Mgmt	End to End/ Transport Layer
Routing/Network	Routing, Least Cost Path	Routing/Network
Data Link Layer	Flow Control, Error Control, Protocol Mgmt	Data Link Layer
Physical Link Layer	Collision Detect, Transmit, Receive	Physical Link Layer

Network Physical Connection

Figure 2.6.   Message path.

base on NODE01. This address, along with the information to transfer, is passed to layer 4 of NODE01.

Layer 4 of NODE01 determines if the data is too large to send in one frame. If so, the layer segments the data and passes the segmented information, now known as a datagram[3], to layer 3. If

[3]A datagram is an entity passed between layers 3 and 4.

the data is within appropriate single-transmission size, the entire piece of data is converted to the datagram and then submitted to layer 3.

Layer 3 adds a header to the datagram consisting of the numeric source and destination addresses of the respective nodes. The layer then determines which data link module is to receive the packet based on the outgoing circuit connected to the respective destination node.

Layer 2 module adds its protocol-related information consisting of framing, synchronization, addressing, and control information as well as a frame check trailer. In such a situation, the respective packet information is appended specifically to the protocol maintained by that module whether it be TCP/IP, DDCMP, SNA, and so forth. At this point, the frame is now ready for transmission to the destination node and is passed to layer 1.

Layer 1 then monitors the line to determine when the line is available for transmission. NODE01 then transmits a preamble to synchronize all physical layers for appropriate frame reception. Layer 1 of NODE01 now transmits the frame over the physical line.

Across the Network

The frame travels on the network to the next adjacent node on the local network. Layer 1 of the respective node receives the message and passes it to the layer 2 module associated with the protocol information of the frame, which then checks the frame for transmission errors. If no errors are detected, the data link header and trailer are removed from the correctly received frame, creating a packet. The packet is then passed up to layer 3, which then checks to see if the local node address matches the destination address in the packet header. If the destination address of the packet is not that of the local node and that node is a routing node, the layer selects the appropriate circuit from its routing table and passes the message back to layer 2 for transmission out of that circuit.

Destination Node

If layer 3 of NODE02 detects that the packet's destination address matches that of NODE02, the layer removes the routing header and passes the datagram to layer 4. The layer examines the header in the datagram for access control purposes. The layer determines if resources are available in order to establish the logical link to PROCB from PROCA. If the respective node has the resources to establish the logical link, it removes the respective header information and passes the connection information to layer 5. If the incoming data was segmented from NODE01, it is reassembled, based on sequence information passed from NODE01, in the layer's receive buffers.

Layer 5 performs all required access control functions in order to determine if the connection request is valid and has the appropriate privileges to be given access to the PROCB. The layer then strips the session control information from the datagram and passes the data to the upper layers of the DNA for PROCB in the user layer. In this situation, a logical link now exists between PROCA on NODE01 and PROCB on NODE02.

COLLISIONS

Under certain circumstances, multiple machines will simultaneously determine that the network is idle. In such a situation, the respective nodes will attempt to transmit a frame to the network simultaneously. This event is known as a collision. This section is for general information purposes only and does not directly apply to the applications in this book; however, some of the information given is important in understanding why some of the requirements for distributed network applications exist.

Before a transmitting node submits a frame to the network, the link management module of layer 2 attempts to avoid a collision by monitoring the carrier sense signal of the physical layer. If the link management module detects traffic on the line, it will wait until the traffic has cleared before another attempt is made for transmission. Once the line is determined to be clear, the physical layer sends an introductory message, known as a preamble, to allow all networked nodes' physical layers to synchronize their clocks. The physical layer then submits the frame to the network and monitors the state of the line for a possible collision.

As the other nodes detect traffic on the line, each node's physical layer notifies the respective data link layer of the traffic to eliminate any transmission conflicts. At this time, the physical layer has received the preamble, so the respective layer synchronizes its clock. The link management module now waits for a frame and collects the data from the physical layer so long as the carrier sense of the physical layer remains active. Once the carrier sense is detected to be no longer active, the link management module assumes that the frame transmission is complete, causing the received frame to be passed to the next layer for appropriate processing.

In order to detect collisions properly, a frame must remain on the line for a specified period of time. Collisions can only occur at the beginning of a frame transmission, known as a collision window, since after that period of time all nodes become aware that the line has been acquired by another node. The collision window is that period during (at least) the first 64 bytes of the frame. Because of this period, the smallest frame allowable is 64 bytes to allow all nodes on the network a chance to acknowledge that a collision has occurred. This adds another interesting feature to collision detection; all receiving nodes process the incoming frame as though it were a standard, error-free frame and do not actively detect collisions as do transmitting nodes. The way that the receiving nodes can detect that a collision has occurred is in the length of the received frame. If the frame is less than the smallest allowable frame, 64 bytes, a collision has obviously occurred on reception.

During a collision, multiple nodes transmit on the line simultaneously, causing the physical layer of the transmitting nodes to activate a collision detect signal. In order to handle a collision, the link management module of the data link layer allows the current frame to continue transmission to allow the other nodes a chance to notice the collision. Once that period has completed, the link management module terminates the transmission and reschedules a second attempt at another time. Each time a collision occurs, the previous steps are reiterated until a specific retry count is exceeded. If, after a number of retries, the transmission is not successful, the frame transmission is canceled.

3

Ethernet Packets

In order to properly understand how to prepare information for transfer between nodes, a basic understanding of the Ethernet frame format is in order. To easily understand the Ethernet frame and how it operates in the DECnet environment, let's compare it to a mailperson and a letter. When a letter is sent, it contains the destination address, source address, and a document. The mailperson goes to each house and compares the destination address of the letter to the address of the house. If they match, the letter is delivered to that house. If the letter is delivered to the wrong address, the letter can be forwarded to the correct address if the person at that house should know the appropriate destination address. If the person at that house does not know the letter's destination, the letter is either discarded or given back to the mailperson for appropriate delivery. Once the letter arrives at the destination address, the person at the destination reads the return address, opens the letter, and reads the document. The return address may now be used to respond to the document if required. It should be noticed that, during the delivery, the letter went to every house on the mailperson's path even though it may not have been delivered, just as a frame on Ethernet goes past each node on its local network path.

Now take the previous example and apply it to the Ethernet

frame format so that a frame can be built. The main ideas to be given here will allow further development in order to implement a customized means of handling information transfer between nodes. In addition to the frame discussed here, there are also a plethora of other frame types available on an Ethernet including, but not limited to, IEEE 802.2 (SNAP), IEEE 802.3 (CSMA/CD), and IEEE 802.4 (Token Bus). In order to provide a foundation as well as remain on track for the implementations outlined in this book, the standard Ethernet frame format will be the center of explanation. To assist in further understanding the Ethernet frame, a utility will be given at the end of this section to allow packet viewing including the source address, destination address, protocol, and user data.

ADDRESSES

The addresses to be utilized for DECNet programming involve a 6-byte, 48-bit string of information that allows identification of the destination and source addresses. The address contains a 32-bit prefix assigned to all nodes with a 16-bit suffix containing the unique identifier of the respective node. End node addresses begin with an AA where addresses with AB in the first byte are multicast addresses. A point to note here is how the addresses are determined to be multicast or explicit. As can be seen, the hexadecimal first byte of an explicit address AA, 0101 0101, has a least significant bit of 0, to the far left. In the first byte of a multicast address AB, 1101 0101, the least significant bit is a 1 with the remainder of the address being a set of values pointing to a group of nodes or a specific node. In the broadcast address FF, 1111 1111, all bits within the entire address are 1. The different combinations of 1s is the designation to the respective controller that the destination address is an explicit, multicast, or broadcast address. See Figure 3.1.

An explicit address contains the address of a single node on a network and is assigned to a node's controller at startup (i.e., AA-00-04-00-56-01), where the LSB of the first byte is a 0. Broadcast addresses are intercepted by all nodes on the network and are predefined to all DNA nodes to denote a set of all nodes (i.e., FF-FF-FF-FF-FF-FF), where all bits are set to 1. A multicast ad-

Explicit Address

```
   AA        00        04        00        56        01
01010101-00000000-00100000-00000000-00011100-10000000
L>>>>>H
```

Multicast Address

```
   AB        00        00        04        56        01
11010101-00000000-00000000-00100000-00011100-10000000
L>>>>>H
```

Broadcast Address

```
   FF        FF        FF        FF        FF        FF
11111111-11111111-11111111-11111111-11111111-11111111
L>>>>>H
```

Figure 3.1.   Address formats.

dress is a multidimensional address accepted by all nodes registered to receive a multicast address (i.e., AB-00-00-04-56-01). In
the multicast address, the LSB of the first byte is 1, while the
remainder of the address is an explicit address denoting one or
more nodes on the network. In order to maintain separation between devices on a network, a separate set of addresses are predefined to different groups containing, for example, end nodes,
while another group contains all routers.

The image in Figure 3.2 depicts a communication configuration representing the relationships between multicasting, broadcasting, and explicit communications for end nodes. As can be
seen, all end nodes are represented by the filled dots and are
contained in circles representing the defined areas for the nodes.
The larger circle represents the entire Ethernet in which the
nodes are contained. In explicit communications, one node can
communicate with one other node on the network by specifying
the destination address in the frame header. In such a situation,
the node with the controller address of the specified destination
address, regardless of the group orientation, will accept the
frame and process it accordingly. In multicasting, several nodes
on the net may simultaneously receive a frame for processing. In

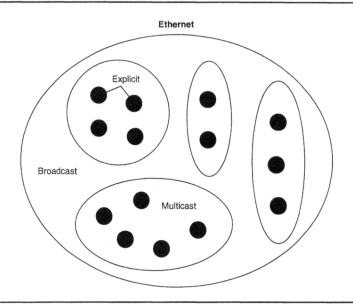

Figure 3.2. Addressing mode relationships.

the diagram, the multicasting groups are depicted by the secondary circles within the larger circle. In such a situation, all nodes within each group may communicate with each other by specifying a multicast address that is registered to all nodes in that group. This representation does not include all the possible configurations for utilizing multicast addresses but it does represent the basic idea of specifying certain addresses for groups of nodes. The broadcast address, the primary circle, allows communications to all nodes within the circle, or local network. This situation overrides all explicit and multicast configurations in that every node in the primary circle receives the frame and processes it accordingly if the node is registered to receive such a frame.

Table 3.1 contains a list of addresses that are applicable to the information outlined in this book. This information has been assembled from experiments involving monitoring the network via custom network monitors in order to view the source and destination addresses of each frame on the network—essentially snooping. The list by no means represents the entire list of available DECNet addresses, but it will provide a basis for additional

Table 3.1. DECNet addresses.

AA-00-04-00-00-00/ AA-00-04-FF-FF-FF	Explicit end node software addresses that may be assigned to each node's controller at startup.
FF-FF-FF-FF-FF-FF	Broadcast address used in a packet's destination address to access *all* nodes.
CF-00-00-00-00-00	Loopback *multicast* address for use in loopback-oriented tests.
AB-00-00-04-00-00/ AB-00-00-04-FF-FF	Multicast addresses for use in nodal multicasting.

research. Further information on DEC-related addresses may be found in the *VMS I/O User's Reference Manual: Part II* (see Bibliography).

PROTOCOLS

In order to allow multiple network-specific processes to operate at a single node, protocols are utilized to identify these individual processes. Such network-oriented processes include TCP/IP, DDCMP, SNA, X.25, or any other related protocol-specific implementation. These identifiers are independent of the addresses and are assigned to each requesting process per channel. This capability adds some interesting possibilities to the ideas that will be given later in this book regarding distributed data processing.

As mentioned earlier, a protocol is a set of common functions that handle certain frames based on the frame's type or protocol identifier. In such a circumstance, the developer may assign a series of protocols to be received by a node in order to allow for specific processing based on the type of protocol. To take this a bit further, assume that several processes exist on the same node. The main problem is the idea of directing packets destined for the node to the appropriate network process. Protocol assignments, by channel, per process, allow the DNA to direct the packet to the destination process without traveling through the entire DNA hierarchy.

To enhance the available information, a compiled list of several available protocols can be found in Appendix A. According to DEC, user-oriented applications may utilize the 0x0660 protocol for initial user application testing; however, it has been found, through researching the different protocols, that user applications can use the different protocols on their network so long as no other applications on the network use that protocol. If there exist several unrelated protocol servers that maintain duplicate protocols on the same network, a major catastrophe can occur (the voice of experience!) where any receiver of the protocol will intercept the frames and attempt to process them, causing unimaginable problems with respective processes.

To provide a better understanding of the use of protocols, let's look at a node that manages several network users (see Figure 3.3). One of the users is based on a TCP/IP protocol and the other user process maintains a DECNet protocol. If the physical layer receives a TCP/IP frame, this frame is passed to the data link module managing the TCP/IP protocol, 0x0008. The frame is stripped of the TCP/IP specific control information, then passed up through the DNA layers to the appropriate destination process. If the physical layer receives a DECNet oriented frame, the

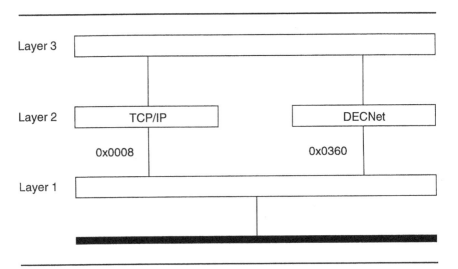

Figure 3.3.   Protocol management.

frame is passed to the module in the data link layer that manages the DECNet protocol, 0x0360. As with TCP/IP, the control information is stripped off and passed up the DNA layers as required. The respective protocol management module is responsible for protocol-specific processing based on the protocol field in the frame. With reference to the Ethernet frame outlined in this book, a general-purpose protocol handler will be presented to provide a better understanding of protocol-related filtering.

PADDING

In order to allow for proper transmission handling under DECNet, Ethernet frames must be at least 64 bytes and cannot exceed 1518 bytes, not including the preamble. Frames less than 64 bytes are assumed to have been involved in a collision, while frames larger than 1518 bytes denote possible equipment problems. As stated earlier, frames being transmitted must remain on the line for a particular period of time in order to properly detect collisions in the respective collision window. Since the control information size is constant, this means that the data portion of the respective frame must be at least 46 bytes. If the data is less than 46 bytes, padding, in the form of NULL characters, is added to the frame to compensate for the minimum size.

If padding is explicitly enabled for a frame, the frame contains a special field that maintains a series of NULL characters to compensate for the minimum required frame size. This field contains the number of characters that allow the frame to equal 64 bytes. Also included in such a frame is a data size field that maintains the number of bytes included in the data field of the frame. In this last instance, the data can be between 0 and 1498 bytes where the receive process uses the size field to determine the number of bytes in the data field of the frame.

In a frame with padding specifically disabled, the data field of the frame may contain between 46 and 1500 bytes. In this instance, there is no special padding field, which means that the padded NULL characters are appended to the data field to compensate for size. One additional change is that the size field, as represented above, is eliminated, which explains the extra two bytes included in the data field of the frame.

ETHERNET FRAME FORMAT

Now that Ethernet frames have been introduced, let's review the frame format itself and examine additional processing-related features associated with the frames. This portion is very important in that it will be used later in this book to explain the creation, submission, and processing of the raw frame information using several methods. For this section a discussion of frames will show the formats of both the padded and nonpadded frames to provide a foundation for frame manipulation. Additional frame formats utilized on a network will not be presented because they have no immediate relevance to the applications to be presented later; however, it is suggested that the reader look further into the IEEE 802.x frames and related functions for additional development and advanced implementations.

No Padding Enabled

In a no-padding situation, the frame contains the basic set of fields to route the frame from a source node to a destination node. As can be seen in Table 3.2 and Figure 3.4, the frame contains a *destination* used to route the frame through the network. This field may contain an explicit, multicast, or broadcast address depending on the implementation requirements. The *source* ad-

Table 3.2.   Ethernet packet without padding.

DESTINATION	Contains the 6-byte destination address of the respective destination that is to receive the packet. May be a multicast, broadcast, or explicit address.
SOURCE	Contains the 6-byte source address of the transmitting node.
PROTOCOL	A 2-byte structure containing the respective protocol relating to the packet.
DATA	A 46- to 1500-byte field for user data. In this instance, NOPAD, the user data is padded to at least 46 bytes.
CRC	A 32-bit CRC based on the address, proto, and data fields.

Dest	Src	Proto	Data	CRC

Figure 3.4.   Ethernet frame with padding disabled.

dress is provided by the source node before transmission to be used at the destination for any required responses or routing tasks. The *proto* field is filled in with the protocol number desired for frame-specific processing at the destination. The *data* field contains the user's data to be transmitted to the receiver at the destination. The *CRC* is calculated by the source node before transmission and is used for error correction at the destination. This field maintains a 32-bit CRC based on the information located in the address, protocol, and data fields of the respective frame.

Padding Enabled

In a padding situation, the packet contains the same basic set of fields as the packet with padding disabled except for two minor changes. As can be seen in Table 3.3 and Figure 3.5, the main differences here are the *count* and *pad* fields. The *count* field contains the number of bytes located in the *data* field, while *pad* contains the padding characters that were previously placed into the data field to compensate for minimum frame size.

PACKET VIEWER

The packet viewer included at the end of this chapter allows viewing of packets as they arrive on the network. Remember that the difference between frames and packets is that frames arrive at the physical layer, while packets are passed from the data link layer to the respective higher modules. The information displayed includes source address, destination address, protocol, and a hexadecimal version of the data itself.

To bring this chapter to a conclusion, let's review some actual packets and associate the given information to tangible data. As can be seen from the packet in Figure 3.6, the source and destina-

Table 3.3.   Ethernet packet with padding.

DESTINATION	Contains the 6-byte destination address to which the packet is to be sent. May be a multicast, broadcast, or explicit address.
SOURCE	Contains the 6-byte source address of the transmitting node.
PROTOCOL	A 2-byte structure containing the respective protocol relating to the packet.
COUNT	A 2-byte count of the number of bytes in the DATA field.
DATA	A 0- to 1498-byte field for user data. In this instance, PAD, the user data field is not padded within the field.
PAD	Contains 0 or more bytes to maintain a minimum packet size.
CRC	The 32-bit CRC based on the frame's contents.

tion addresses are the same. For this particular example, the protocol is 0xDF81, which represents a NETBIOS-related protocol. Now refer to the hexadecimal view of the packet as well as the size of the packet. It can be seen that the packet size is 60 bytes where NULL characters are filled after the user data to make the packet the minimum size required by DECNet. At this point you are probably wondering why 64 bytes was previously given as the minimum packet size while here it is shown that the packet is 60 bytes. Don't forget to take into account the 32-bit, 4-byte, CRC field of the packet. This information is not passed to this user-oriented process upon reception.

Dest	Src	Proto	Count	Data	Pad	CRC

Figure 3.5.   Ethernet frame with padding enabled.

```
RECEIVING
D: 0  0  c6 0  a  b4 / S: 0  0  c6 0  a  b4 / P: 81-df / S: 60
0  0  c6 0  a  b4 0  0  c6 0        . . Æ . .  ´ . . Æ .
a  b4 81 df 0  0  0  0  0  0        . ´ . ß . . . . . . .
0  0  0  0  0  0  0  0  0  0        . . . . . . . . . . .
0  0  0  0  0  0  0  0  0  0        . . . . . . . . . . .
0  0  0  0  0  0  0  0  0  0        . . . . . . . . . . .
0  0  0  0  0  0  0  0  0  0        . . . . . . . . . . .
```

Figure 3.6.   Ethernet packet 1.

The packet in Figure 3.7 shows a legitimate source and destination address with a DECNet protocol and a size of 60 bytes (i.e.,
64). For further investigation, compare the addresses and protocol
to the hexadecimal view of the packet—quite interesting! It should
be noticed that the first 12 bytes match the destination and source
addresses, respectively. The next two bytes contain the protocol
representing the DECNet protocol of 0x0360. In the data portion
of the packet there exists routing information as well as the NULL
characters to compensate for the 46-byte minimum data field size
of the packet.

In both instances, padding was disabled, forcing the NULL
padding at the end of the data field of the packet. Notice also that
the respective size field is not available, which, once again,
points to the fact that the packet is not a padded packet. For
reference, the size of the packet was extracted from the return of
the respective network I/O function.

```
D: aa 0  4  0  33 6  / S: aa 0  4  0  30 6  / P: 60-3 / S: 60
aa 0  4  0  33 6  aa 0  4  0         ª . . . 3 . ª . . . .
30 6  60 3  0  0  0  0  0  0         0 . ` . . . . . . . .
aa 0  4  0  33 6  0  0  aa 0         ª . . . 3 . . . ª .
4  0  30 6  0  0  0  0  60 99        . . 0 . . . . . ` .
20 9f 60 38 84 f4 17 ff 2  83        . ` 8 . ô . . . . .
0  0  0  0  0  0  0  0  0  0         . . . . . . . . . . .
```

Figure 3.7.   Ethernet packet 2.

```c
/*VIEWPACKET.C*/
#include <descrip.h>
#include <stdio.h>
#include <iodef.h>
#include <string.h>
#include <ctype.h>

/*Extracted from SYS$LIBRARY:LIB.REQ*/
#define NMA$C_STATE_ON  0              /* Respective State On  */
#define NMA$C_STATE_OFF 1              /* Respective State Off */

#define NMA$C_PCLI_PTY 2830           /* Protocol                              */
#define NMA$C_PCLI_PRM 2840           /* Promiscuous mode                      */
#define NMA$C_PCLI_BFN 1105           /* Number of receive buffers             */
#define NMA$C_PCLI_BUS 2801           /* Receive Buffer Size                   */
#define NMA$C_PCLI_PHA 2820           /* Port Address                          */
#define NMA$C_PCLI_FMT 2770           /* Packet Format Mode                    */
#define NMA$C_PCLI_PAD 2842           /* Padding Mode                          */
#define NMA$C_PCLI_HWA 1160           /* Respective Hardware Address           */
#define NMA$C_PCLI_EKO 2847           /* Echo Mode                             */

#define NMA$C_LINMC_SET 1             /* Set Port Address                      */
#define NMA$C_LINMC_CLR 2             /* Clear Port Address                    */
#define NMA$C_LINMC_SDF 4             /* Set Port Address to DECNet Default    */

#define NMA$C_CTLIN_LBE 1041          /* Local Error Counter                   */
#define NMA$C_CTLIN_OVR 1064          /* Overrun Counter                       */

#define NMA$C_LINFM_ETH 1             /* Ethernet Packet Format                */
```

```c
int status;
short channel;
short iosb[4];        /*Simplified IO status block for discrete display        */
unsigned char buffer[1500];

/*------------------------------------------------------------------------------
/* controller()
/*------------------------------------------------------------------------------
/* Hit each controller name until one "responds" then set the channel mode.
/*------------------------------------------------------------------------------*/
void controller()
{

    char device[5][6] = {"XEA0:", "XQA0:", "ESA0:", "ETA0:", "*"};
    int i, status;

    struct
    {
        short    BFN;
        long     BFN_VAL;
        short    PTY;
        long     PTY_VAL;
        short    BUS;
        long     BUS_VAL;
        short    PAD;
        long     PAD_VAL;
        short    PRM;
        long     PRM_VAL;
        short    ETH;
        long     ETH_VAL;
```

```
} startupbuffer =
    {
        NMA$C_PCLI_BFN, 2,                              /* Number of Buffers    */
        NMA$C_PCLI_PTY, 0x0360,                         /* DECNet Protocol      */
        NMA$C_PCLI_BUS, 1500,                           /* Buffer Size          */
        NMA$C_PCLI_PAD, NMA$C_STATE_OFF,                /* Padding Mode OFF     */
        NMA$C_PCLI_PRM, NMA$C_STATE_ON,                 /* Promisc Mode ON      */
        NMA$C_PCLI_FMT, NMA$C_LINFM_ETH                 /* Ethernet Format      */
    };

struct                              /*Startup buffer size and address struct    */
    {
        int  size;
        int  addr;
    } startupbufferdescriptor =
        {
            sizeof(startupbuffer),          /*Size of buffer            */
            &startupbuffer                  /*Address of startup buffer */
        };

                                        /* Device name descriptor */
struct dsc$descriptor_s devicedescriptor = { 0, DSC$K_DTYPE_T, DSC$K_CLASS_S, 0};

                                        /* Assign the device */
for (i=0, status = 0; (status != 1) && (device[i][0] !='*') ; i++)
    {
    devicedescriptor.dsc$a_pointer = device[i];
    devicedescriptor.dsc$w_length = strlen(device[i]);
    status = sys$assign(&devicedescriptor, &channel, 0, 0);
    }
if (!(status & 1)) lib$stop(status);
```

```c
     printf("Controller %s\n",device[i-1]);

                                    /* Start the controller channel and set the      */
                                    /* respective mode                                */
     status = sys$qiow(0, channel, IO$_SETMODE + IO$M_STARTUP + IO$M_CTRL,iosb, 0, 0, 0,
          &startupbufferdescriptor, 0, 0, 0);
     if (!(status & 1)) lib$stop(status);
     if ((iosb[0] & 1) != 1)
     {
       printf("STARTUP ERROR (Hex) : %x %x %x %x\n",iosb[0], iosb[1], iosb[2], iosb[3]);
       exit(iosb[0]);
     }
}

/*-----------------------------------------------------------------------------------*/
/* readether()                                                                        */
/*-----------------------------------------------------------------------------------*/
/* This function simply reads the packets outputting the data to the screen          */
/*--------------------------------------------------------------------------------*/
int readether()
{
  int i,j;

  printf("RECEIVING\n");
  while(1==1)
  {
                                    /*Header information is received in               */
                                    /*P1 and body of packet is in P5                  */
     status = sys$qiow(0, channel, IO$_READLBLK, iosb, 0, 0,
```

41

```c
    &buffer[14], sizeof(buffer)-14, 0, 0, &buffer[0], 0);

if (!(status & 1))
{
    lib$stop(status);
}

if (iosb[0] != 1)                    /*If IO error, exit and display IOSB    */
{
    fprintf(stderr, "STATUS : %x %x %x\n", iosb[0], iosb[1], iosb[2], iosb[3]);
    lib$stop(iosb[0]);
}

                                     /*Extract address, protocol and size info   */
                                     /*Size is given by adding the size of the    */
                                     /* header (14) to iosb[1]                     */
printf("D: %x %x %x %x %x / S: %x %x %x %x %x / P: %x-%x /    S: %d\n",
    buffer[0],buffer[1],buffer[2],buffer[3],buffer[4],buffer[5],
    buffer[6],buffer[7],buffer[8],buffer[9],buffer[10],buffer[11],
    buffer[12],buffer[13],iosb[1] + 14 );

for(j=0;j<(iosb[1] + 14 );j+=10)
{
    printf("%2x %2x %2x %2x %2x %2x %2x %2x %2x %2x    ",
        buffer[j],buffer[j+1],buffer[j+2],buffer[j+3],buffer[j+4],
        buffer[j+5],buffer[j+6],buffer[j+7],buffer[j+8],buffer[j+9]);

    for(i=0;i<10;i++)
```

```c
            {
                if(!isprint(buffer[j+i]))
                {
                    buffer[j+i]='.';
                }
            }

            printf("%c %c %c %c %c %c %c %c %c %c\n",      /*Print the data portion of the packet      */
                buffer[j],buffer[j+1],buffer[j+2],buffer[j+3],buffer[j+4],
                buffer[j+5],buffer[j+6],buffer[j+7],buffer[j+8],buffer[j+9]);
        }
    }
}

/*---------------------------------------------------------------
/* main()
/*---------------------------------------------------------------*/
main()
{
    controller();
    readether();
}
```

4

Network Programming Basics

One of the most discouraging areas of network programming to those new to the area is finding all of the available facts and being able to filter out the superfluous information. One thing that was noticed when actual development began on test implementations was that there is not a lot of work involved in actually developing a basic implementation, as will be seen later. The majority of the work involves using the basic information and implementations to develop a full system that utilizes the information provided here. At this point, several aspects of DECNet programming have been covered, including a general overview of networks and the basic formats and contents of Ethernet frames. The final topics to cover before actually delving into network applications include VMS-related functions for performing network I/O and some basic information regarding the Ethernet controller and drivers.

SYSTEM SERVICES

One very important fact that deserves reiteration is that there is not really a lot of work required to implement a basic set of processes in order to perform interprocess communications over a network. One reason for this is that VMS provides a set of functions that are callable from VAX C or any other DEC language and that perform a majority of the work required for proper network I/O. VMS System Services are a set of procedures that the operating system uses to control process resources, provide a means of performing interprocess communications, and provide process I/O support as well as a plethora of other programming-oriented utilities. During standard operations, it should be noticed that the operating system utilizes these same functions that are available to the programmer, which means that the programmer has access to many of the *black box* features of the system. A perfect example of System Service usage is in outputting data to a terminal where a System Service call outputs a specified block of information to SYS$OUTPUT.

All System Service functions may be called using the standard VAX procedure calling convention in which each parameter required by the function is passed based on the requirements of the parameter within the function. As will be seen, calling a System Service function from VAX C is just as straightforward as calling a C function with a few minor exceptions, of course, which will be seen later. For basic network-oriented operations, there are only five functions that are required by any network process: SYS$ASSIGN, SYS$SYNCH, SYSQIO, SYSQIOW, and SYS$DASSGN. As the reader becomes more proficient in network-oriented programming, additional calls may be utilized as seen fit by the developer to enhance the end product. For information on additional System Service calls, it is recommended that the *VMS System Services Reference Manual* (see Bibliography) be consulted. The other important fact to remember is that the basic implementation of each function does not change drastically between applications, which makes the basic ideas of network programming easy to understand and easy to port between applications. As stated by DEC, since these calls are VMS calls and not directly related to DECNet Phase IV or V, the VMS calls are dependent on the upgrade compatibility of VMS and not on the networking software.

I/O Status Block

The I/O Status Block is a structure utilized to maintain the return values of I/O function calls. This structure can be used to determine the completion status of the operation, determine

```
typedef struct
{
    short  cond_value;  /*Condition of the operation    */
    short  count;       /*Number of bytes transferred   */
    int    info;        /*Information flag              */
}
io_statblk;
```

Figure 4.1.   I/O Status Block structure.

the number of bytes transferred, or determine if a transfer error has occurred as well as the parameter that caused the error. Once the respective I/O function has completed execution, the status block is passed to another function to determine the condition and completion status of the operation as well as provide a textual result of the operation. See Figure 4.1.

The *cond_value* is a word value containing the return status condition of the operation such as SS$_NORMAL, SS$_CONNECFAIL, or SS$_PROTOCOL. Defines such as those named are located in the SSDEF.H header file and are dependent on the respective device. For more information on the defines associated with a particular operation and device, refer to the VMS manual associated with that device as well as the *VMS I/O User's Reference Manual Part I* and *Part II*. The sample code for this section, to be presented later, outlines methods for determining the textual condition of the operation. The *count* word contains the number of bytes transferred during the respective I/O operation. The *info* field is an additional application-oriented status field that is dependent on the respective operation being performed. Note that the use of the status block may vary slightly for each System Service call, which means that the *info* field should be appropriately defined for the respective operation.

Link Assignment

Before communicating with any device on the local node or any process on the network, a logical link must be established to allow data transfer between the devices and/or processes. The function that performs this operation is called SYS$ASSIGN and is one of the standard VMS System Service calls.

```
return = SYS$ASSIGN(task, channel, accessmode, mailboxname)
```

The link assignment function SYS$ASSIGN performs a request for connection to the task. The task, known as a task specification string, is passed as a descriptor, defined in DESCRIP.H, and may contain a device or a process identification on a local or remote node. The task specification is outlined for each application presented to provide the flexibility and understanding of the respective application. During this link assignment, the function receives a *channel* number as a reference to a short integer corresponding to the logical link assigned to the task or device outlined in the task parameter. This channel is to be used in future calls in order to send and/or receive data with the remote task or device.

The *accessmode* is a longword value that represents the access mode related to the respective channel. I/O operations on the channel can only be performed from equal and more privileged accessing processes/users. This information is used during access management to the respective remote node for the remote object or local device. In order to set the respective process access mode to that of the calling process, set this parameter to 0.

The *mailboxname* is the descriptor containing the logical name of the mailbox to be associated with the task. If SYS$ASSIGN is used for nontransparent communications, a mailboxname is required since nontransparent communications is, in its basic form, based on mailboxes. In a situation that utilizes mailboxes, the SYS$CREMBX System Service call is utilized in order to create a channel to the mailbox where that channel is used in all subsequent I/O function calls. For those applications that utilize transparent interprocess communications or device-specific operations, a 0, the default value, is placed in this parameter. Transparent communications include, for all practical purposes, all applications outlined in this book that perform direct I/O between processes.

The *return* value of the function returns the status of the call as a longword condition and is defined in the SSDEF.H header file. This information may then be passed to the LIB$STOP function in order to get a VMS textual error value for the respective numeric longword value.

Information Transfer

Once a channel is established between the processes or between a process and a device, the process may transfer information over that channel with the partner device or process. The SYS$QIO[W] System Service function performs information preprocessing, then queues the information to the device or process at the opposite end of the channel. The way that this operation occurs is by using the information passed to the SYS$QIO function to create an I/O request package. The request package is a structure allocated from the system's nonpaged dynamic pool and placed into the I/O request queue for transport to the target located at the opposite end of the channel. Upon completion of the respective I/O function, the request has been properly serviced, an event flag is set, and/or an asynchronous system trap service routine is called.

The function definitions of SYS$QIO and SYS$QIOW are identical in every respect except for how the function returns. SYS$QIO, the asynchronous version, submits the I/O request on the respective channel and returns immediately upon servicing the respective I/O request. This routine allows flexibility in the way in which returns are handled; however, it is advised that either an event flag be associated with the function or an AST be called in order to handle the return properly. SYS$QIOW, the synchronous version, is identical to the SYS$QIO function call except that it waits for the completion of the respective request. The order of operation within the function issues a SYS$QIO immediately followed by a SYS$WAITFR System Service to wait for the event flag. Determining which function to use depends on the desired operation and whether the function should return immediately in an asynchronous manner or operate synchronously.

```
return = SYS$QIO
(eventflag,channel,function,iostatusblock,astadr,astprm,p1,p2,p3,p4,p5,p6)

return = SYS$QIOW
(eventflag,channel,function,iostatusblock,astadr,astprm,p1,p2,p3,p4,p5,p6)
```

The *eventflag* is a longword value assigned to the respective function that is used to allow additional function calls based on that flag. Each successive call may monitor the flag in order to allow determination of the completion status of the respective SYS$QIO function. This flag is cleared when the function is called and set when the operation completes. If this parameter is not required it should be set to 0.

The *channel* is the short integer value assigned in the SYS$ASSIGN call. This value is used to notify the SYS$QIO function which link, or channel, to utilize in performing the function. For example, in order to send a message for a virtual device, the function short-integer parameter may contain IO$_WRITEVBLK where receiving a message uses the IO$_READVBLK modifier. Function defines may be found in the *VMS I/O User's Reference Manual* and may be included in the source with the IODEF.H header file. Other function definitions allow for communication with different devices, setting device modes, and retrieving device counter information as well as related communication operations. Other such I/O functions include IO$_READPBLK/ IO$_WRITEPBLK for physical I/O as well as IO$_READLBLK/ IO$_WRITELBLK for logical I/O.

The *iostatusblock*, as outlined above, is a quadword structure used to receive the final completion status of the operation. This information does indeed vary between applications and will be explained for each application provided in this book.

The *astadr* is an asynchronous system trap (AST) service routine to be executed when the operation completes and contains the address of the respective function with a return type of integer. An AST is a routine that needs to be executed by a process and executes by interrupting the process when triggering events, such as I/O completion, occur. The *astprm* parameter is a longword argument passed to the AST service routine as the parameter to the respective routine. These two parameters work together to provide a means of *firing* a routine immediately after the respective function has completed. This may be utilized for post-I/O processing in order to capture the information immediately before and after exchanging data over the channel.

The parameters *p1,p2,p3,p4,p5,p6* vary between implementations and are device/function-specific depending on the actual implementations. This information, as with the I/O status block, will be explained for each implementation; however, additional implementations require different buffer combinations and are referenced in the *VMS I/O User's Reference Manual Part I* and *Part II*.

The *return* value of the function returns the status of the call as a longword condition and is defined in the SSDEF.H header file. This information may then be passed to the LIB$STOP function in order to get a VMS error textual value for the respective numeric longword value.

Input/Output Synchronization

The SYS$SYNCH System Service call allows asynchronous services to complete in a synchronous manner. Under normal circumstances, the event flag of associated functions may be monitored by using the SYS$WAITFR function call; however, during I/O, additional monitoring is required. As applied to I/O, the process may implement a SYS$QIO function, which is an asynchronous function, and immediately call the SYS$SYNCH function. This will ensure that the respective I/O operation has completed by monitoring the eventflag used in the respective I/O function call as well as the information in the I/O status block.

```
return = SYS$SYNCH ( eventflag, iostatusblock)
```

The only parameters are *eventflag* and *iostatusblock*. The eventflag is the event flag assigned in the prior call to the SYS$QIO function for data transfer. This function may also be applied to other System Service functions, but for I/O it is applied specifically to the SYS$QIO function. The I/O status block is utilized in maintaining the results of the respective call by allowing follow-up checks on the number of bytes transferred, the resultant status, and related function results.

The reason that the process may need to utilize the SYS$SYNCH call is, first of all, to force an asynchronous SYS$QIO into a synchronous communications function. This separation of functionality allows for more control over the function by the process concerning error detection; however, a simple call to SYS$QIOW is much easier to implement. The decision is left entirely up to the programmer; however, the options are available for implementing the same function several different ways to add flexibility for the programmer.

Deassigning a Link

The SYS$DASSGN function deassigns the channel that was established in SYS$ASSIGN and was utilized in all intermediate I/O System Service function calls. This function clears the linkage and related control information in order to free resources that are no longer required. If any I/O requests were made prior to this call and have not been requested for input, the transfer is terminated. The only parameter for the function call is the *channel* that was previously established in the SYS$ASSIGN System Service function.

```
SYS$DASSGN(channel)
```

It is very important here to note that if two processes are communicating over the shared channel, a synchronous type of deassignment is recommended. Such synchronicity is created when both processes cooperate in the channel deassignment to ensure that all resources for both processes are deallocated. Under several circumstances it was found that if the partner process (i.e., the one located at the other end of the channel from the primary process) is not told of the deassignment and does not terminate accordingly, the partner process will reach a state where it simply waits for the data to be transferred over the channel in a complementary service request.

As can be seen in Figure 4.2, each connected process should cooperate in the link termination. One method of handling deassignment is to issue a termination message from a primary process to the respective partner process. The partner processes the message and returns an acknowledgment to the primary process. Once both processes understand that the link is to be terminated, each process calls to the SYS$DASSGN System Service function, then exits appropriately. This method provides a neat and clean method to perform resource deallocation and provides

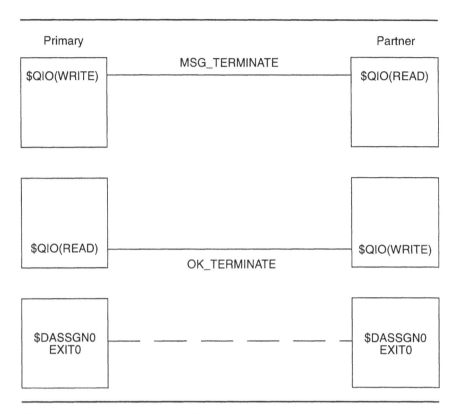

Figure 4.2.   A link termination scenario.

a proper exit for both associated processes. In a situation where a process is connected to a device, synchronous deassignments are not required because the device will handle its own disconnect. The process only needs to issue one call to SYS$DASSGN per connected channel.

CONTROLLER MODES

In order to implement certain low-level network-oriented functions, the calling process must set the controller into a specific mode. The reason for setting the mode of the controller is to perform operations that are specific to the implementation at hand. This is accomplished immediately after initializing the channel via SYS$ASSIGN over the respective channel utilizing a call to

SYS$QIO. The three primary modes to be discussed here are promiscuous mode, protocol filter mode, and multicast filter mode. An additional section included later outlines an explicit addressing mode; however, this is associated with the protocol filter mode and maintains a difference by the means in which the information is processed.

Before assigning a mode, the respective controller *name* must be known. Each type of controller is assigned a respective name to access that controller for all future operations as well as assigning a channel to that controller. For DEUNA and DELUA devices, the name is XEA0:, for devices DEQNA and DELQA, the name is XQA0:, DEBNA is ETA0:, while DESVA devices is ESA0:. For the applications provided in this book, ESA0: was utilized; however, modifications may be made to the code to adjust for the devices available in the host machine.

Promiscuous Mode

In any dictionary, the term promiscuous means *accepting any and all*. As applied to network-related operations, promiscuous is a controller mode where the node will accept any and all frames that arrive at the controller on the network. The primary advantage of this mode of operation is in the area of network management and monitoring. In such a state, a process may intercept all frames on the network, provided that timing is appropriate to do so, and, for instance, calculate the percentage utilization of the network as well as the busiest nodes on the network. Essentially, in this mode, the user process may intercept any frame information from the network regardless of the destination node of the frame. Note that direct operations on the frames within the promiscuous process will cause the process to lose frames. Ideal configurations include shared images and global sections where the network process operates independently from the frame processor.

The major drawback to such an implementation is that only one promiscuous mode channel may be assigned per node on the network at any given time. This relates to the idea of multiplexing every frame within one particular node to multiple processes. The other negative aspect of this mode is that the controller must process every frame that is on the network, which adds more load to the respective node's processor.

Protocols Filters

Processes may be attached to the DNA in a way that specifies the protocol that is to be directed to that process. These identifiers are independent of the processes and are assigned on a per-channel basis. In this instance, the receiver processes may register on a machine as a receiver of, for example, protocol 0x0660, which means that all related protocol receivers on the network will accept any frame with that protocol. Essentially, a process exists for a particular protocol, and that process waits until that protocol is given to it by the DNA before performing any processing. A *protocol filter* is the name given to this mode since it allows the local node to filter through all frames with the named protocol. This mode is only useful if promiscuous mode is in the OFF state because promiscuous mode overrides all related specific filters.

In Figure 4.3, there are three processes attached to the DNA hierarchy. Every process maintains the same address by way of the respective node, but each maintains a different protocol iden-

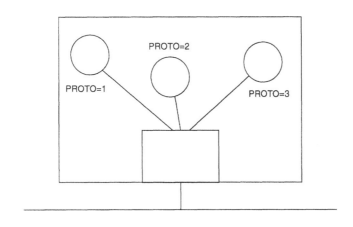

Figure 4.3. Protocol filter assignments to multiple processes.

tification. In such a case, whenever the node receives an appropriate frame, it will accept the frame and forward it to the process registered with the protocol given in the frame. One idea this depiction presents is that of identifying separate protocols for each process, which is one method that heads in the direction of distributed processing. It is possible to share one protocol assignment so long as the explicit address for each assigned channel is unique for each node. When registering for shared protocols, the respective protocol must be shareable at the destination node and, as stated, each address per channel must be unique on that node. If an attempt is made to register several processes to one protocol without appropriately establishing that protocol as shareable, the secondary registering processes will return a "bad parameter" error. For further information regarding shared protocols, refer to the *VMS I/O User's Reference Manual: Part II*.

Multicast Filters

A multicast filter allows a node to accept the multicast addresses registered by its respective network-oriented processes. The filter is utilized in a manner similar to the means utilized by layer 3 of the DNA hierarchy as well as the way in which protocols are filtered. All nodes that are enabled to receive multicasts will read the destination address of the frames on the network and, if the destination address matches the node address or any multicast address registered, pass the frame to the respective registered process. The one thing to keep in mind here is that *every* machine on the local network having a registered receiver that is to receive the said multicast address will receive that one frame simultaneously. This introduces an interesting idea of data distribution without repeated frame submissions to the multitude of possible receivers on the network.

As can be seen in Figure 4.4, one machine may have a number of processes attached to the DNA, which may maintain different multicast addresses. There may be one process that registers, for example, two multicast addresses. Each address corresponds to a particular *group* of processes relating to a particular function across the network. The image depicts a situation where one process can receive a multicast address destined for addresses 2 or 5.

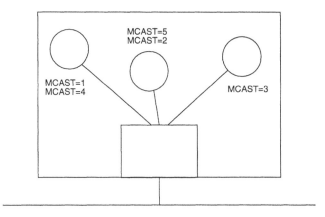

Figure 4.4.   Multicast address registration for three separate processes.

This example is an extreme case; under most circumstances, there will usually be one process that retrieves several multicast frames or, if several processes are available, different methods will be implemented to differentiate between the incoming frames. There are many different implementations available for multicasting filters as well as different configurations for the respective process/ node groups. This section is merely a simple introduction into one area of network communication paradigms.

LOOPBACK TEST

To demonstrate some of the methods given in this chapter, the following source code provides a loopback process that writes a frame to the network utilizing protocol 0x0090 and a loopback assistance multicast address of CF-00-00-00-00-00. The purpose of this application is to submit a frame and wait for a response from any node on the network. Once the response is received, the resultant frame header is printed to the screen. The sequence is repeated continuously until 100 loopback tests have been produced or the user exits the process.

```
SENDING
RECEIVING
Checking
D: aa 0 4 0 58 6 / S: aa 0 4 0 fa 5 / P: 90- 0
SENDING
RECEIVING
Checking
D: aa 0 4 0 58 6 / S: aa 0 4 0 fa 5 / P: 90- 0
SENDING
RECEIVING
Checking
D: aa 0 4 0 58 6 / S: aa 0 4 0 fa 5 / P: 90- 0
SENDING
RECEIVING
Checking
D: aa 0 4 0 58 6 / S: aa 0 4 0 fa 5 / P: 90- 0
SENDING
RECEIVING
Checking
D: aa 0 4 0 58 6 / S: aa 0 4 0 fa 5 / P: 90- 0
SENDING
RECEIVING
Checking
D: aa 0 4 0 58 6 / S: aa 0 4 0 fa 5 / P: 90- 0
```

Figure 4.5.   Loopback test output.

As can be seen in Figure 4.5, the process sends a frame to the network, then checks for a response. Once any response is received at the node, it is printed to the output device. Notice that the destination address is always the same. The source node of the response frame (FA-05) extracts the source node of the originating frame (58-06) in order to respond properly to the loopback request. Another interesting point to notice is that the responding node submits a frame with a protocol value of 0x0090, which matches the loopback protocol assigned to the original frame issued by the originating process.

```
/*LOOPBACK.C*/

#include <descrip.h>                /*String descriptor types          */
#include <stdio.h>                  /*Standard Input Output header      */
#include <iodef.h>                  /*Input Output definitions          */
#include <string.h>

/*Extracted from SYS$LIBRARY:LIB.REQ*/
#define NMA$C_STATE_ON 0            /* Respective State On              */
#define NMA$C_STATE_OFF 1           /* Respective State Off             */

#define NMA$C_PCLI_PTY 2830         /* Protocol                         */
#define NMA$C_PCLI_PRM 2840         /* Promiscuous mode                 */
#define NMA$C_PCLI_BFN 1105         /* Number of receive buffers        */
#define NMA$C_PCLI_BUS 2801         /* Receive Buffer Size              */
#define NMA$C_PCLI_PHA 2820         /* Port Address                     */
#define NMA$C_PCLI_FMT 2770         /* Packet Format Mode               */
#define NMA$C_PCLI_PAD 2842         /* Padding Mode                     */
#define NMA$C_PCLI_HWA 1160         /* Respective Hardware Address      */
#define NMA$C_PCLI_EKO 2847         /* Echo Mode                        */

#define NMA$C_LINMC_SET 1           /* Set Port Address                 */
#define NMA$C_LINMC_CLR 2           /* Clear Port Address               */
#define NMA$C_LINMC_SDF 4           /* Set Port Address to DECNet Default */

#define NMA$C_CTLIN_LBE 1041        /* Local Error Counter              */
#define NMA$C_CTLIN_OVR 1064        /* Overrun Counter                  */

#define NMA$C_LINFM_ETH 1           /* Ethernet Packet Format           */
```

```c
int status;
short channel;                          /*Simplified IO status block for discrete display        */
short iosb[4];
unsigned char buffer[1500];

/*-----------------------------------------------------------------------------
/* controller()
/*-----------------------------------------------------------------------------
/* Open the ethernet controller.
/*-----------------------------------------------------------------------------*/
void controller()
{
    char device[5][6] = {"XEA0:", "XQA0:", "ESA0:", "ETA0:", "*"};
    int i, status;

    struct
    {
        short   BFN;
        long    BFN_VAL;
        short   PTY;
        long    PTY_VAL;
        short   BUS;
        long    BUS_VAL;
        short   PAD;
        long    PAD_VAL;
        short   PRM;
        long    PRM_VAL;
        short   ETH;
        long    ETH_VAL;
```

```
} StartupBuffer =
    {
    NMA$C_PCLI_BFN, 2,                  /* IO Buffers to allocate   */
    NMA$C_PCLI_PTY, 0x0090,             /* Loopback protocol        */
    NMA$C_PCLI_BUS, 1500,               /* Size of IO Buffer        */
                                        /* Frame padding is OFF     */
    NMA$C_PCLI_PAD, NMA$C_STATE_OFF,
                                        /* Promiscuous mode OFF     */
    NMA$C_PCLI_PRM, NMA$C_STATE_OFF,
                                        /* Ethernet packet format   */
    NMA$C_PCLI_FMT, NMA$C_LINFM_ETH
    };

struct                                  /*Startup buffer size and address struct   */
    {
    int size;
    int addr;
    } StartupBufferDescriptor =
    {
    sizeof(StartupBuffer),              /* Startup buffer size      */
    &StartupBuffer                      /* Address of startup buffer */
    };

                                        /* Device name descriptor   */
struct dsc$descriptor_s devicedescriptor = { 0, DSC$K_DTYPE_T, DSC$K_CLASS_S, 0};

                                        /* Assign a device to the controller   */
for (i=0, status = 0; (status != 1) && (device[i][0] != '*') ; i++)
    {
```

```c
        devicedescriptor.dsc$a_pointer = device[i];
        devicedescriptor.dsc$w_length = strlen(device[i]);
        status = sys$assign(&devicedescriptor, &channel, 0, 0);
    }

    if (!(status & 1)) lib$stop(status);
    printf("Controller %s\n",device[i-1]);

                            /* Issue a startup and mode for controller      */
    status = sys$qiow(0, channel, IO$_SETMODE + IO$M_STARTUP + IO$M_CTRL,iosb,
            0, 0, 0, &StartupBufferDescriptor, 0, 0, 0, 0);
    if (!(status & 1)) lib$stop(status);
    if ((iosb[0] & 1) != 1)
    {
        printf("Startup Error : IOSB = 0x%2x %2x %2x %2x\n",
                iosb[0], iosb[1], iosb[2], iosb[3]);
        exit(iosb[0]);
    }

}

/*------------------------------------------------------------------*/
/* checkwriteether()                                                */
/*------------------------------------------------------------------*/
/* This function simply reads the packet outputting the data to the screen */
/*------------------------------------------------------------------*/
int checkwriteether()
{
    int     i;
```

```c
    printf("Checking\n");                          /* Read the data into a local buffer        */

    status = sys$qiow(0, channel, IO$_READLBLK, iosb, 0, 0,
                      &buffer[14], sizeof(buffer)-14, 0, 0, &buffer[0], 0);

                                                    /*Output the response                       */
    printf("D:%2x %2x %2x %2x %2x/S:%2x %2x %2x %2x %2x/P:%2x-%2x\n",
           buffer[0],buffer[1],buffer[2],buffer[3],buffer[4],buffer[5],
           buffer[6],buffer[7],buffer[8],buffer[9],buffer[10],buffer[11],
           buffer[12],buffer[13]);

    if (!(status & 1))                              /* Display error if one occurs at this point */
    {
            lib$stop(status);

    }

    if (iosb[0] != 1)                               /* If the status block shows an error        */
    {                                               /* write the respective output               */
            fprintf(stderr, "iosb = %2x %2x %2x %2x\n", iosb[0], iosb[1], iosb[2], iosb[3]);
            lib$stop(iosb[0]);

    }

    return (iosb[1] + 14);                          /* Return bytes transferred                  */

}

/*--------------------------------------------------------------------------
/* writeether()
/*--------------------------------------------------------------------------
/* This function writes a coded loopback packet to the ethernet
/*--------------------------------------------------------------------------*/
int writeether()
{
```

```c
    int     i;

    char    xmtp[8]        =        /* Loopback mcast adrs and protocol */
            {0xcf,0x00,0x00,0x00,0x00,0x00,0x90,0x00};
    char    xmtbuf[14]     =        /* Message to send in data          */
            {0x00,0x00,0x02,0x00,
             0xaa,0x00,0x04,0x00,0xf6,0x05,
             0x00,0x00,0x01,0x00};

    printf("SENDING\n");

    status = sys$qiow(0, channel, IO$_WRITELBLK, iosb, 0, 0,  /* Write */
        &xmtbuf[0], sizeof(xmtbuf), 0, 0, &xmtp[0], 0);

    if (!(status & 1))
    {
        lib$stop(status);
    }

    if (iosb[0] != 1)               /* If the status block shows an error */
    {                               /* write the respective output        */
        fprintf(stderr, "iosb = %2x %2x %2x %2x\n", iosb[0], iosb[1], iosb[2], iosb[3]);
        lib$stop(iosb[0]);
    }

    return (iosb[1] + 14);          /* Return the number of bytes          */
}
```

```
/*---------------------------------------------------------*/
/* main()                                                  */
/*---------------------------------------------------------*/
main()
{
    int i;

    controller();
    for (i=0;i<100;i++)
    {
        writeether();
        checkwriteether();
    }
}
```

5

Transparent Interprocess Communications

Task-to-task communications is a feature inherent in all DECNet-oriented operations. Essentially, it allows multiple processes to communicate over logical links by requesting link-oriented operations through layer 4 of the DNA. These network-oriented functions set up logical links, receive logical link requests from remote nodes, send data, receive data, and terminate the logical link. One interesting feature of VMS-specific task-to-task functions is that they are language-independent and may be called from within any VMS language that translates into operating system dependent commands. The functions available to perform transparent interprocess communications, TIPC, allow processes to initiate a link, exchange messages, and terminate the link. Everything is available in the VMS System Service function calls, which can be found on VMS-related nodes.

PHASES OF TIPC

One of the most frustrating parts of implementing TIPC for the first time is that of trying to understand how it can be accomplished. This section will outline the three phases involved in TIPC in a very simple and straightforward manner. There may be deviations from this sequence for functionality but, in the long run, the sequence must be followed for optimum results. In the following sections, the phases of Initiation, Transfer, and Termination will be explained to provide a basis for the remainder of the chapter.

TIPC Initiation

In order to begin a session, a local process must initiate a logical link to another task on a remote, or local, node before information transfer can begin. From the view of the processes, the logical link is seen as a numeric representation, a channel, for the link. This can be compared to picking up a telephone and dialing the phone number to connect to another person. When the person at the other end picks up the phone, the link is established and the conversation can begin. The link, in this case, is established by notifying the local node about the task name and remote node to which the source task will connect. This task specification is accomplished by defining a task specification string to state the remote node and process name for connection with the primary process.

The format for the task specification string is TASK= TASKSTRING, where TASKSTRING is the name of the node, device, and the partner task on either the local or a remote node. The string may also contain the username and password for access purposes to the partner process; however, a proxy log-in is preferred for security purposes. In the case of calling the process executable directly, the executable must be in the SYS$LOGIN directory of the respective remote node log-in. For cases where the executable is located in a directory other than SYS$LOGIN, a DCL COM file may be created to accommodate the network startup.

Another method for declaring a remote task is to define the remote task as an object on the remote node. This essentially eliminates the elaborate task specification strings. As is shown in Figure 5.1, the Network Control Program, NCP, is used to add the object to the network object database. The first line is used to set up the name of the object to access on the node and will replace the entire task specification string outlined above. The second line defines the file that is represented by the object name.

```
edward & NODE01> ncp set object asynch -
_edward & NODE01> file disk0:[edwd]asynch2-x.exe -
_edward & NODE01> user edward -
_edward & NODE01> pass edpwrd -
_edward & NODE01> number 0
```

Figure 5.1.   Object definition.

This represents the information outlined for the task specification string format outlined in Table 5.1. The next two lines define the username and password for appropriate access to the account on the remote machine. The final line is a numeric value between 0 and 255 that represents the number of the object.

Now that the information has been added to the network object database, the information can be viewed for verification pur-

Table 5.1.   Task specification strings.

TASK = NODE01::ASYNCH2-X.EXE	The remote process executable is in SYS$LOGIN of NODE01.
TASK = NODE01::ASYNCH-2.COM	The remote process executable is not in SYS$LOGIN of NODE01; a COM file starts the executable. The COM file would read: $run disk0:[xxxx]asynch2- x.exe
TASK = NODE01"UNAME PWORD"::xxxx	This version takes into account that a proxy login does not exist but may utilize one of the two previous samples.
TASK = NODE01::ASYNCH	This final version utilizes an entry into the network object database.

```
edward & NODE01> ncp sho kno obj

Known Object Volatile Summary as of 1-JUN-1991 20:08:30

    Object  Number   File/PID                      User Id Password

    $IPCACP      0    00000084
    $MOM         0
    $NICONFIG    0
    PCX$SERVER   0    SYS$COMMON:[SYSEXE]PCX$SER
    SMISERVER    0    00000090
    ASYNCH       0    DISK0:[EDWD]ASYNCH2-X.EXE   EDWARD EDPWRD
    THRUPRT_NET  0    00000091
    X$X0         0    00000095
    FAL         17    FAL.
```

Figure 5.2. NCP object listing.

poses. As is shown in Figure 5.2, the NCP command issued in Figure 5.1 is reflected by the definition of the object listed in the network database. Note that the use of the NCP SET command will place the entry into the volatile database while an entry using NCP DEFINE will place the object definition into the permanent database.

A task may also be specified as a system logical or a hard-coded string within the main process. Of the two, a VMS logical is much easier to handle since the logical may be changed, instead of the code, in order to initiate a different task; however, additional coding is required to locate the appropriate task name in the VMS logical tables. The implementations outlined in this book will utilize a hard-coded string defined within the respective process and will use the remote process's node and name for access.

Once the task is defined and the primary process is started, the local layer 4 will take the local request and pass it to the remote node. The remote node's layer 4 will verify that the requested object exists and that the log-in information from the requesting node is valid. If the link request and object information are correct, the request is sent to the target object, which causes the target object, or process, to initialize. The initialized process is registered with a process name identified by NET_xxxx in the process list and issues an acknowledgment to the connection request through the task specification string specified with SYS$NET. SYS$NET is essentially a return handshake to the connect request. At this point, a channel exists that now connects the primary process and the destination remote process. If at any time during this process the link is rejected by the remote object, or process, the requesting object receives a link reject error and aborts the operation.

An important factor is to determine which process is to initiate communications. The reason for this decision is that the initiating process will initialize the process outlined in the task specification string and establish a link with the task. This is quite useful because the programmer, or user, does not have to be concerned with the order of startup operations for the application. The programmer/user only needs to start the process determined to initiate the channel, the primary, for complete TIPC initialization while the system handles the startup and connection of the partner task. Another important factor to take into consideration is that only one channel may be established for I/O between two processes; however, multiple channels may exist for one process connecting to several related partners.

TIPC Transfer

The transfer of information to a remote process over the logical link is the primary purpose of TIPC. Once the connection is established, the next step is, logically, to initiate transfer of information between the processes over the channel established in the Initiate phase. The primary idea to keep in mind in this type of interprocess communication is that each process must cooperate in the transfer of the information. When one process issues a request to send information, the other process must issue a request to receive information. Layer 4 of the transmitting node will not send the information until layer 4 of the partner process issues a request to receive the information. This adds a form of synchronicity to the idea of TIPC where each respective process must be prepared to perform a corresponding action in response to its network partner.

TIPC Termination

Termination involves simply deallocating the resources given the network partners for use in TIPC. The main operation involves requesting termination through DECNet, which causes the channel to drop. One thing to keep in mind is which process is to terminate the connection, while another consideration is a means of terminating the remote process when the channel is terminated. As stated earlier, a synchronous type of disconnect is recommended in order to properly deallocate the links and associated resources for the primary and partner processes.

TIPC IMPLEMENTATION

In the following TIPC implementation, the three phases of TIPC will be reviewed with actual code samples written in VAX C. During each section, the previously outlined information will be detailed in order to parallel the code given in the figures.

TIPC Initiation

In order to establish a connection between processes, the task specification string must be passed to the VMS System Service function SYS$ASSIGN within the primary process. This function, if successful, will establish a channel between processes for transfer and will initialize the remote task identified in the task specification string. Once the remote task is initialized, it must call the SYS$ASSIGN function with its task specification string set to SYS$NET. This will provide an acknowledgment that the process has initialized and that layer 4 should complete the link back to the primary process. The SYS$NET definition, which is for all practical purposes a logical path back to the primary process, is initialized when the primary process requests a connection.

The code depicted in Figure 5.3 outlines a simple function to access a channel easily. The function requires that the task specification string and a variable (by reference) for the channel be passed to the function. The function will then assign the task specification string to a VMS descriptor (DESCRIP.H). The de-

```
int EstablishChannel(char *TASK(), short *channel)
{
        register status;
        struct dsc$descriptor terminal;

        /*Assign the task spec str to a descriptor     */
        terminal.dsc$w_length = strlen(TASK);
        terminal.dsc$b_dtype = DSC$K_DTYPE_T;
        terminal.dsc$b_class = DSC$K_CLASS_S;
        terminal.dsc$a_pointer = TASK_ID;

        /*Assign a channel to the task                  */
        if((status = SYS$ASSIGN (&terminal, channel, 0, 0))
           & 1) != 1)
        {
                LIB$STOP(status);
        }
        return(1);
}
```

Figure 5.3.   Establishing a channel.

scriptor is then passed to the system call with the status and channel being returned. If an error should occur, LIB$STOP will halt the process and return the textual nature of the problem. In an actual implementation, LIB$STOP may be replaced by a return value in order to notify the caller of an error instead of halting the process completely. As can be seen, the center of the function EstablishChannel() is a call to the VMS System Service function SYS$ASSIGN. For this implementation SYS$ASSIGN requires the parameters for the task specification string and a variable in which to return the established channel number. This channel number is used for later calls to transfer information between the respective network processes.

TIPC Transfer

Once a channel has been established between a primary task and a partner, information may then be transferred between the two processes. This is accomplished through the SYS$QIO or SYS$QIOW VMS System Service functions. The only requirements for using this function are that a channel has been established and that the message to transmit does not exceed 256 bytes. There are alternatives to transmitting larger messages; however, this document will not detail that option to any great detail.

In this implementation, information transfer is performed by calling the SYS$QIO System Service function followed by a call to SYS$SYNCH. The only information required is the channel received during Initiate, the information to transfer and the size of the information to transfer. In Figure 5.4, the operations involve transmitting a message to the process connected over the channel assigned during the Initiate phase. The call to SYS$QIO attaches the I/O event to flag 1, which is used in subsequent function calls within the TransmitMessage() function. It then places a request to layer 4 to transmit the message located in the buffer over the channel to the partner previously designated in the task specification string.

Once the request has been placed, the function then calls the SYS$SYNCH function to monitor the I/O status block and event flag 1 for a completion status. This function will wait until the I/O operation initiated in SYS$QIO has completed and returned without an error in the return status.

The final step of the function is to review the condition field of the I/O status block for any possible errors. If at any step of TransmitMessage() an error should occur, the function will pass the resulting status to the LIB$STOP function so that VMS may halt the process and issue a message regarding the error.

In the parameter line of TransmitMessage(), an AST function may be passed to the SYS$QIO function for execution after the SYS$QIO function has completed. This function may be a function that performs post-processing on the information. If no function is required, it may be supplanted by a NULL.

The ReceiveMessage() implementation, depicted in Figure 5.5, is nearly identical to the TransmitMessage() function except for the fact that the I/O operation is set up to receive any messages currently available on the channel. The way to determine the direction of the I/O is through the use of flags passed to the

```
int TransmitMessage(short channel, buffer message,
    int (*AST_FUNC()))
{
  register status;
  io_statblk status_block;

  /*Request to xmit message*/
  if(((status=SYS$QIO(1, channel, IO$_WRITEVBLK,
      &status_block, AST_FUNC, &status_block,
      message, sizeof(buffer), 0, 32, 0, 0)) & 1) != 1)
  {
      LIB$STOP(status);
  }

  /*Wait for completion of operation*/
  if(((status=SYS$SYNCH(1, &status_block)) & 1) != 1)
  {
      LIB$STOP(status);
  }

  /*Check for iostatusblock errors*/
  if((status_block.cond_value & 1) != 1)
  {
      LIB$STOP(status_block.cond_value);
  }

  return(1);
}
```

Figure 5.4.   TransmitMessage TIPC function.

respective SYS$QIO operation. As can be seen in Figure 5.5, the function is set to IO$_READVBLK, which tells layer 4 to read a block from the link specified by the channel number. Recall that in the TransmitMessage() function the respective I/O function is set to IO$_WRITEVBLK.

As with TransmitMessage(), once the I/O operation has completed, the information is placed into the buffer. The size of the buffer is used in both functions to notify VMS of the size of the available buffer to allocate in order to place the information arriving from the remote process/object. Another similarity is that

```
int ReceiveMessage(short channel, buffer message,
    int (*AST_FUNC()))
{
  register status;
  io_statblk status_block;

  /*Request to receive message*/
  if(((status=SYS$QIO(1, channel, IO$_READVBLK,
      &status_block, AST_FUNC, &status_block,
      message, sizeof(buffer), 0, 32, 0, 0)) & 1) != 1)
  {
      LIB$STOP(status);
  }

  /*Wait for completion of operation*/
  if(((status=SYS$SYNCH(1, &status_block)) & 1) != 1)
  {
      LIB$STOP(status);
  }

  /*Check for iostatusblock errors*/
  if((status_block.cond_value & 1) != 1)
  {
      LIB$STOP(status_block.cond_value);
  }

  return(1);
}
```

Figure 5.5.   ReceiveMessage TIPC function.

an AST function address may be passed to the function in order
to perform post-processing on the incoming information.

TIPC Termination

In order to perform an orderly disconnect, the VMS System Service function SYS$DASSGN is called with the parameter being
the channel to disconnect. The channel referenced is the same
channel assigned in Initiate and used for information transfer
during the Transfer phase. See Figure 5.6.

```
int Disconnect(short channel)
{
  register status;

  /*Request to deassign a link*/
  if(((status=SYS$DASSGN(channel)) & 1) != 1)
  {
      LIB$STOP(status);
  }

  return(1);
}
```

Figure 5.6. Disconnect TIPC function.

When a process issues a SYS$DASSGN for a channel, it does not terminate the partner process. This function simply disconnects the logical link, frees the channel, and frees the resources associated with the link. In order to terminate partner processes properly, it is suggested that the primary process send a message to the partner that the channel is to be disconnected. Once received, the partner will deassign the channel and exit, as will the primary process once the message is acknowledged. This method of disconnection performs an orderly and synchronous deassignment in order to make a clean break for all processes involved.

SAMPLE APPLICATION

The sample provided here is a simple derivation of the standard Hello World program with which every programmer should be familiar. The objective of this application is to start a remote task and volley a simple sentence. The one catch to this implementation is that the only way to terminate is to stop the primary and the remote tasks separately. Since neither the Disconnect() nor SYS$DASSGN functions are called, the system will handle the cleanup of all allocated resources. For reference, the sample uses a Bicyclic Messaging technique, which will be detailed later in this chapter. The complete application code is provided at the end of the chapter.

```
#include     "[edward.ipc]ipc.inc"
#include     <stdlib.h>
#include     <stdio.h>
```

Figure 5.7.   Primary task includes.

Primary Task

The primary task is responsible for initiating the link, initializing the remote task, and initiating the message transfer. As can be seen in the code fragment in Figure 5.7, the code contains a statement to include a file, ipc.inc, which contains the four functions outlined previously for interprocess communications.

To demonstrate AST functions, the code segment depicted in Figure 5.8 defines two functions that are passed to the TransmitMessage() and ReceiveMessage() functions. These functions, as stated earlier, are called after the respective I/O has completed, which in this case prints completion messages based on the I/O function performed.

The section depicted in Figure 5.9 is the main() function of the code. This section maintains local declarations for I/O buffers, the I/O channel, and the task specification string. The buffers for the sample are 200-character vectors that allow maintenance and transfer of general structures.

The call to EstablishChannel() establishes a channel to the remote task that is to be the partner of the primary. During this call, the function is passed the task_id, defined as ASYNCH2-X.COM on NODE01, as well as a reference to the channel that is

```
int AST_XMIT(io_statblk *write_status)
{
    printf("ASYNCH1 AST Post Transmit\n");
}

int AST_RCV(io_statblk *write_status)
{
    printf("ASYNCH1 AST Post Receive\n");
}
```

Figure 5.8.   Primary task AST routines.

```
main()
{
    buffer   outtext, intext;
    short              channel;
    int                        AST_PROC();
    char               task_id[] = "NODE01::\"TASK = ASYNCH2-x.COM\"";

    printf("ASYNCH1-x : Establishing Link to ASYNCH2-x\n");

    if(!EstablishChannel(task_id, &channel))
    {
        printf("ASYNCH1-x LINK : Unable to Establish Link\n");
    }

    strcpy(outtext,"Hello to ASYNCH2-x from ASYNCH1-x");
    for(;;)
    {
        printf("ASYNCH1 to ASYNCH2 - HELLO THIS IS A TEST\n");
        if(!TransmitMessage(channel, outtext, AST_XMIT))
        {
            printf("ASYNCH1-x TRANSMIT : Unable to Transmit via Channel\n");
        }

        if(!ReceiveMessage(channel, intext, AST_RCV))
        {
            printf("ASYNCH1-x RECEIVE : Unable to Receive via Channel\n");
        }
        printf("ASYNCH2-x to ASYNCH1-x %s\n\n",intext);
    };
}
```

Figure 5.9.   Primary task main().

established between the two processes. The task referenced in task_id is a DCL COM file located in the SYS$LOGIN of the respective account on NODE01. The COM file simply contains one line stating *$run [edward.examples]asynch-2.exe* to initialize the partner executable. If the channel is not established to the partner, a negative response will be issued to the initiating primary process, causing an error message to be displayed to the user.

The primary process then prepares its outtext by copying "Hello to ASYNCH2-x from ASYNCH1-x" to the buffer. The TransmitMessage() function is then called with references to the channel, outtext buffer, and the respective AST function. Once the function returns successfully, the AST will be called, printing the output to the screen. The process then proceeds to perform a ReceiveMessage() by passing the same channel, intext buffer, and the AST. Once the ReceiveMessage() function returns, the AST prints accordingly and the process prints the result of the receive from the remote task.

Remote Task

The remote task is responsible for acknowledging the connection request and for maintaining orderly communication with the primary task. As can be seen in the code fragment of Figure 5.10, the same file is included in order to allow calls to the interprocess communications functions. The AST functions are also declared, as with the primary task, in order to allow a post-I/O function to be executed.

Defined in the main() function (Figure 5.11) of the remote

```
#include"    [edward.ipc]ipc.inc"

int AST_XMIT(io_statblk *write_status)
{
    printf("ASYNCH2 AST Post Transmit\n");
}
int AST_RCV(io_statblk *write_status)
{
        printf("ASYNCH2 AST Post Receive\n");
}
```

Figure 5.10.   Remote process includes and AST routines.

```
main()
{
    buffer   outtext, intext;
    short              channel;
    int                AST_PROC();
    char               task_id[] = "SYS$NET";
    FILE               logfile = fopen("ASYNCH2-x.LOG", "w+");

    if(!EstablishChannel(task_id,&channel))
    {
        fprintf(logfile,"ASYNCH2-x LINK : Unable to Establish Link\n");
    }

    for(;;)
    {
        if(!ReceiveMessage(channel, intext, NULL))
        {
            fprintf(logfile,
            "ASYNCH2-x RECEIVE : Unable to Receive via Channel\n");
        }

        sprintf(outtext,"%s / Back to ya from ASYCNH2-x",intext);
        if(!TransmitMessage(channel, outtext, AST_XMIT))
        {
            fprintf(logfile,
            "ASYNCH2-x TRANSMIT : Unable to Transmit via Channel\n");
        }
    }

    fprintf(logfile,"\n ASYNCH2-x Complete \n");
    fclose(logfile);
}
```

Figure 5.11.   Remote process main().

81

task are two buffers for storage of the I/O with the primary task as well as the channel that is to be used in transferring the communications. The first element to notice is that of the task specification string defined in task_id. The task_id is referencing SYS$NET in order to acknowledge the connection request by the primary task.

The other element to notice in this process is the order of operations during I/O. Recall that the first I/O operation executed in the primary task is a TransmitMessage(). Recall as well that the communicating tasks must cooperate in the communications; when a transmit request is issued by one process, a receive request must be issued by a second process to transfer the message along the channel. In the remote task, the complementary I/O request is issued first to allow the message to move along the channel from primary to remote.

The next step in this process is to transform the received message in intext into another message to volley back to the primary task. As can be seen, "/ Back to ya from ASYCNH2-x" is appended to the end of the received message and sent back to the primary. As with the previous explanation of the I/O transfer function and its complement, TransmitMessage() is called in the remote process where ReceiveMessage() is called in the primary to accept the message.

Primary Task Output

Now that the source code has been reviewed for the primary and remote tasks, let's review the output of the primary task sequence and see what happens during each step.

PARADIGMS

Now that the basics have been presented, it is time to explain how this implementation may be applied to legitimate applications. This section will provide generic situations where this implementation may be used; however, while these paradigms may not represent the best situations in which to implement TIPC, they will provide a means of understanding how TIPC can be implemented for future applications.

Table 5.2.   Output from TIPC session for primary task.

Output	Operation
ASYNCH1-x: Established Link to ASYNCH2-x	The primary has requested a channel to the ASYNCH2-x.COM.
	Remote end-to-end communications issues a call to ASYNCH2-x.COM, which in turn starts ASYNCH2-x.EXE.
	ASYNCH2-x.EXE has returned a call to SYS$NET to acknowledge.
ASYNCH1 to ASYNCH2— HELLO THIS IS A TEST	ASYNCH1-x is preparing to transmit a message to ASYNCH2-x.
ASYNCH1 AST Post Transmit	The primary performs a TransmitMessage while the remote performs a ReceiveMessage.
ASYNCH1 AST Post Receive	The remote performs a TransmitMessage while the primary performs a ReceiveMessage.
ASYNCH2-x to ASYNCH1-x Hello to ASYNCH2-x from ASYNCH1-x / Back to ya from ASYNCH2-x	The received message from the remote is printed to the screen.

Peer-to-Peer

A peer/peer application would be a situation where independent processes operate on separate nodes but need to maintain some type of contact with each other. This type of situation may also be compared to a parallel scenario where multiple processes maintain independence while still transferring status information to the other connected processes. See Figure 5.12.

An example application would be one where there exists a primary operating system with a remote partner system whose state is dependent on the primary. In such a situation, a peer process would exist on the host machine connected to a peer process lo-

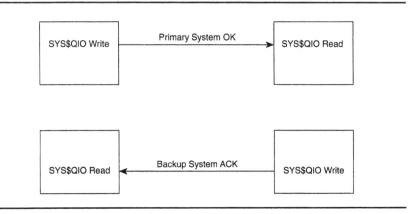

Figure 5.12.   Peer-to-peer configuration.

cated on the partner machine. Recall from previous explanations regarding DECNet that a peer-to-peer scenario is one in which no one entity has complete control over the other while each maintains the ability to communicate directly with one another.

During normal operation, the peers transfer status messages to each other at regular intervals or as the status changes. If, at any time, a negative status is transferred from the host system's peer to the partner system's peer, the partner system would execute a particular event in response to the negative status. When the host system's peer returns a positive status to the backup system's peer, the partner system would respond accordingly.

With respect to TIPC (Figure 5.13), the systems would be configured in such a way as to allow two-way communications over the logical link between the two processes. PROCA on NODE01 occasionally sends a request to PROCB on NODE02 to check the status of the respective node. During each respective request, PROCA issues a TransmitMessage() while PROCB issues a ReceiveMessage(); then PROCA cycles to a ReceiveMessage() function and waits for information to arrive over the channel. When PROCB responds, it issues a TransmitMessage() to PROCA, which is already waiting for the information.

In this circumstance, as depicted in the ReceiveMessage() and TransmitMessage() functions, it is best to issue a SYS$QIO followed by a SYS$SYNCH in order to determine the status of the

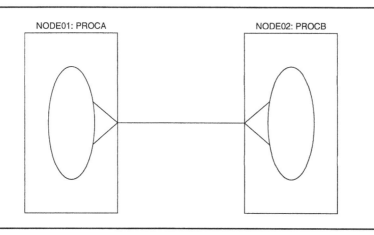

Figure 5.13.   Single-channel peer-to-peer.

link easily. If at any time the link should drop, indicating a failure of either PROCA or PROCB, SYS$QIO will return a failure status. At this point, the process receiving a failure message will know that the partner machine has failed, allowing the local machine to take over the operation.

As can be seen in Figure 5.14, if a failure is detected in transmitting or receiving a message, for this implementation it is assumed that the link has dropped. In such a case, the process that detected the drop should take over the processing activities and attempt to revive the link. This is accomplished by following the message transfer function with a Disconnect() function call to clean up the residue of the dropped channel immediately followed by an EstablishChannel() call to reestablish a link. Once the link is reestablished, the process should return processing activities to the other process as required.

Client/Server

A client/server or client/monitor paradigm exists in an environment where there exists a client process that sends requests to the server/monitor. The second part of the paradigm is built around the difference between a server and a monitor. A server is an active process that services requesting clients but may also

```
for(;;)
{
    if(!ReceiveMessage(channel, intext, NULL))
    {
        .
        .
        /*Takeover Processing Activities */
        .
        .
        Disconnect(channel);
        if(!EstablishChannel(task_id, &channel))
        {
            .
            .
            /*Error recovery*/
            .
            .
        }
    }

    if(!TransmitMessage(channel, outtext, AST_XMIT))
    {
        .
        .
        /*Takeover Processing Activities */
        .
        .
        Disconnect(channel);
        if(!EstablishChannel(task_id, &channel))
        {
            .
            .
            /*Error recovery*/
            .
            .
        }
    }
}
```

Figure 5.14. Sample peer I/O.

provide initiating messages, while a monitor is a passive server and only services client requests without any initiating messages.

The most useful implementation for this paradigm is that of a data server. In such an application the server would reside on a system that maintains some type of data storage or gathering entity. The remote client, or series of clients, would send requests to the server to retrieve information for remote processing. A simple example would be a data server located "as" the front end for a data interface in a production environment. The server process would be located on the host with an interface to the production entity database. The client processes are located on several remote machines to provide a dynamic graphical interface. Each display update cycle, each client would send a message corresponding to an entity or database entry. The server would inspect this message, retrieve the desired data, and transfer the information back to the client for a dynamic update of the interface. See Figure 5.15.

There are two easily understandable methods for implementing such a system. One method is to utilize the client/monitor type of implementation where the monitor is under control of the

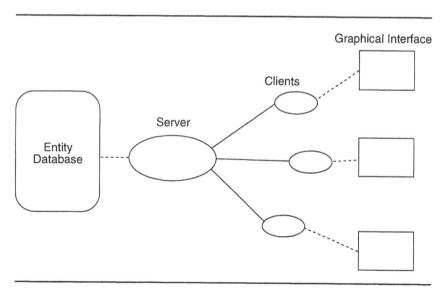

Figure 5.15.   Client/server.

clients. The clients actively request information from the monitor in order to update the user interface. The second possible method is through the use of a client/server paradigm where the server actively polls the clients and/or sends information as the information is updated in the database. This situation would also allow clients to make requests for information required from the server.

With respect to TIPC, the server process must maintain a logical link to each client process. A simple implementation would make the server process the primary while each respective client process represents the remote partner of the primary. To implement this type of situation, the server will be told of all client processes before startup. On startup, the primary sequences through each client, initializing the link and performing local initialization for future operations.

As can be seen in Figure 5.16, the sample server maintains an array of client-related information including the task specification string and a variable to maintain the respective channel to the remote client. The server process sequences through the array, initializing each client and storing the returned channel in the client's channel. During I/O, the application loops through the array issuing a ReceiveMessage() followed by a TransmitMessage() for a client along the client's channel. Likewise, the client must first issue a TransmitMessage() followed by a ReceiveMessage().

This type of situation demonstrates the use of an active server, which polls each client for data and submits data to the client during each poll. If no data is available in either direction, a health check should be performed in order to verify the integrity of the client and associated link to the client.

DEVELOPMENT

The development phase of a TIPC system requires that several factors be determined and that some basic ground rules be established. A few of the factors to take into account are contention, messaging, message processing, primary process, and the number of channels. These are only general factors that should be taken into account in ground-up development work; however, the needs of the individual project will differ. The samples provided are not

```
struct
{
  char    task_id[20];
  int     channel;
}task_struct[20];

int     i,NumberOfClients;

{
  .
  .
  .
  /*Load the client task specification information */
  .
  .
  .
}

for(i=0;i<NumberOfClients;i++)
{
  EstablishChannel(task_struct[i].task_id, &task_struct[i].channel);
}

for(i=0;i<NumberOfClients;i++)
{
    if(!ReceiveMessage(task_struct[i].channel, intext, NULL))
    {
      .
      .
      .
    }

    if(!TransmitMessage(task_struct[i].channel, outtext, AST_XMIT))
    {
      .
      .
      .
    }
}
```

Figure 5.16.   Sample server implementation.

the only two methods available; however, they will provide the reader with experience to expand to more complex methods.

During a sequence of message transferrals between processes, it becomes necessary to monitor which process has control of or needs control of the channel. If not properly monitored, the processes could be placed into contention for the channel, and under some circumstances it could result in a deadlock. The reason that contention for the channel can occur is that, as previously mentioned, a process must make an active request to send a message while the partner must make an active request to receive the message. If no complementary request is made or if two similar requests are made, the processes will, for all practical purposes, hang.

Bicyclic Messaging

Bicyclic Messaging implements an equal and opposite read/write scheme for information transferral. In this method, the primary process initiates a SYS$QIO write on startup followed by a SYS$SYNCH. The partner process initiates, on startup, a SYS$QIO read followed by a SYS$SYNCH. The next step in each process is to switch the direction of information transfer (i.e., primary reads, partner writes). See Figure 5.17.

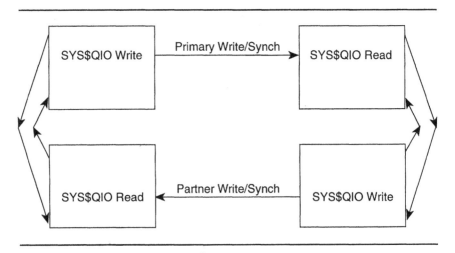

Figure 5.17.   Bicyclic messaging.

The advantage to this type of TIPC is that of simplicity. This is by far the simplest and most robust form of TIPC to implement. There are no problems involved in contention since each process takes its turn on the channel. The only problem involved with this type of situation is that of the messaging system's flexibility. Unsolicited messaging in this type of implementation is impossible since each respective process must wait until its own time to send and/or receive information from the other process.

Queued Subprocesses

This method of messaging requires several additional processes to send and receive messages along with a shared commons for shared queue storage. The theory behind this method lies entirely in the fact that there exists one process entirely dedicated to transmitting messages to its remote receive partner and another dedicated to receiving messages from its remote transmitter partner. Both the transmit and receive processes sport a queue capable of maintaining the messages in association with the main process. The main process, which is used for data manipulation, processes incoming and outgoing information without the need to be concerned about receiving or sending messages. All of the information that it requires from its network partners exists in the shared receive queue, while all of the messages to be sent are placed in the shared transmit queue for handling by its subprocesses. See Figure 5.18.

The primary advantage to this form of messaging lies in the fact that all messaging is essentially unsolicited. Either process group may send or receive information at any time. The receiver's purpose is to wait until its remote transmitter partner sends information; it then places this information on the receive queue for access by the main process sharing its queue. Since the main process is not concerned with waiting for messages, as with Bicyclic Messaging, this process may tend to the duties for which it was written. Another interesting advantage to this paradigm is that of hibernation. When the primary process has no messages on its input queue, it may hibernate since it is essentially inactive. This allows the CPU more time to tend to other processes in the system. When a message is available on the input

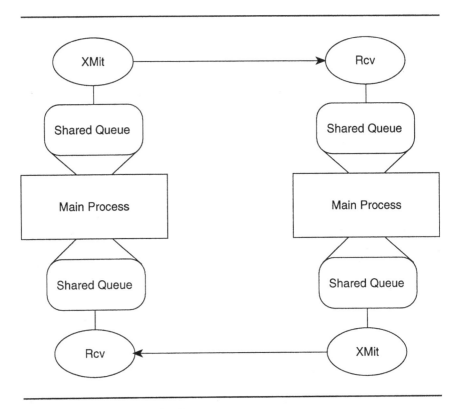

Figure 5.18.   Queued subprocesses.

queue, the receive subprocess can send a SYS$WAKE to the main process.

Messaging and Message Processing

In a messaging system, it is evident that some means of identification is required where different types of structures may be transferred across the network between partner processes. To implement this correctly, it is important to properly identify the required types of messages that will be sent and to take into account what types of responses will be produced according to the message type. See Figure 5.19.

```
struct message
{
    int type; /* Identifies the type of message */
    void *buffer; /* Message */
    int target_node;/* The message destination proc*/
}
```

Figure 5.19.   Sample messaging structure.

The ideal, and simplest, message structure will allow for the entry of a message identifier, a generic pointer to the actual message, and a target node identifier. The target_node is used in multilayered TIPC systems, which provides for propagation of the message through each process to the destination, or target, process. Once a process receives such a message, the information can be sent directly to a processing function, which strips the message down and processes the message based on its *type*. See Figure 5.20.

PRIMARY PROCESS

The primary process is responsible for the initialization of a connection with the partner process. This is important to decide since this will determine the initial state of the overall system. A

```
int Process(struct message msg)
{
    switch(msg.type)
    {
        case 1 : {
                    /*code*/
            }
        case 2 : {
                    /*code*/
            }
    }
}
```

Figure 5.20.   Sample message processing code.

second factor to take into account when determining which process is to be primary is the location of the process. The primary process should be easily accessible and located on the primary machine involved in a system. These are just initial judgments and will probably be modified from application to application.

CONNECTING CHANNELS

While developing a TIPC system, the programmer must decide on how many different processes will be involved with the system. If two processes are involved, then of course there will exist one channel; however, when multiple processes are involved, the situation becomes a bit more complex.

In a two-process system, the processes must simply maintain a link without contention. The system must also provide for an orderly message-passing structure and processing system. If more than two processes are to be used, additional factors are taken into account, such as the primary process, whether the main primary will initiate all partners or will there be subprimaries to initiate the partners, which process will initiate the message transferral, and which type of messaging paradigm should be used.

TWO PROCESSES

The overall implementation of a two-process system is simple. The main factors involved are determining which is the primary process and which messaging paradigm to implement. See Figure 5.21.

Primary Process

This decision is left entirely up to the programmer. It is best to determine the accessibility and load per process. The primary process should be the process located on a central or primary machine and the process maintaining the heaviest or most centralized information flow.

Messaging Paradigm

This decision is based entirely on the amount of information and whether the processes will produce and/or require unsolicited

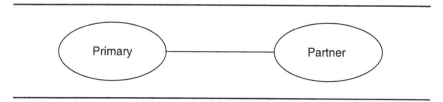

Figure 5.21.   Two processes, one link.

messages. For minor message traffic and no unsolicited messages, the simplest method to implement is Bicyclic Messaging. This method will provide a clean and robust method of data transfer.

In a situation involving two processes, it may be overkill to implement the Queued Subprocess paradigm; however, if the primary is required for heavy processing, it may be best to implement this paradigm. In such a situation, the load of message management and propagation is maintained by the subprocesses. The main processing portion of the entities can perform the processing on the messages and related functions as required, leaving the transfer-oriented functions to the transmit and receive subprocesses.

MORE THAN TWO PROCESSES

Implementing a system with more than two processes involves more thought than the simple two-process system. The programmer must take into account which process is primary, whether there will be multiple subprimaries with control over a portion of the partners, whether there will be one primary with control over all partners, and the message loading on the system.

Messaging Paradigm

In a system where more than two processes exist, care must be taken to determine how a message will be propagated. It would be extremely difficult to implement Bicyclic Messaging unless there was only one primary process. Bicyclic Messaging applies virtually only to information transfer between two processes, and it would take a considerable amount of time to propagate a message through each set of subprimaries and available partners.

In a situation where there may be a lot of heavy messaging

traffic or where unsolicited messages may be required, it is best to implement the Queued Subprocess paradigm. In such a situation, the load of message management and propagation is maintained by the subprocesses. The main processing portion of the system can retrieve and propagate messages as needed through the shared queues without having to wait for the messages to be sent or received in a message loop.

One Primary

Using one primary for multiple partners is a simple implementation; however, this can cause some incredible loading on the primary process assuming that there exists a large number of partners. In using any of the aforementioned messaging paradigms, the primary would have to maintain a channel for every partner. Message propagation and determining the appropriate destination of the return message from the primary in such an implementation are not major factors since each message can be tied to the respective channel or queue. See Figure 5.22.

Subprimary Processes

The use of subprimaries relieves some of the load from the main primary process. This type of scenario would allow one primary

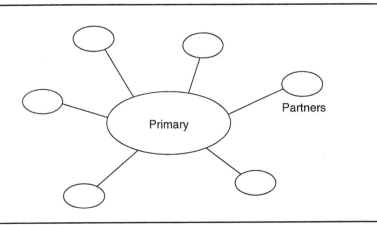

Figure 5.22. Multiple processes, one primary.

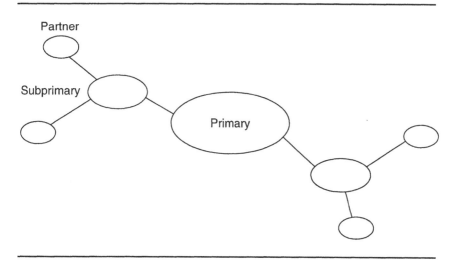

Figure 5.23.   Multiple process, subprimaries.

to maintain a channel or queue for a few partners/subprimaries; then each subprimary would maintain a channel or queue for each of its partners/subprimaries. Messaging would be accomplished via propagation through subprimaries until the destination process is reached. See Figure 5.23.

In using Bicyclic Messaging, the main problem encountered is that of message propagation. Since Bicyclic Messaging is designed around two processes connected by a single channel, each pair of connected processes would only be able to transfer messages during each messaging cycle. Assuming that there exist several layers of several partners each, and the primary is transferring a message out to the farthest partner, the propagation delay would be the limiting factor. See Figure 5.24.

The most efficient means of propagating messages is through the use of the Queued Subprocess model. In this situation, the main process of each processing group has no effect on the transmit and receive subprocesses of each processing group. All message propagation is handled within the subprocesses, which also allows for unsolicited message transfer. An argument for the use of subprimaries is that each respective subprimary may be used as a filter for the main process. Based on the target process defined in the respective message, the subprocesses may forward

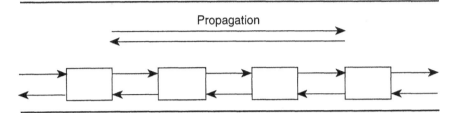

Figure 5.24.   Bicyclic messaging multiprocess message propagation.

messages through each subprimary without intervention from the main process. A preprocessing situation may be established between the main primary and the subprimaries, thus additionally reducing the overall processing required by the main primary. See Figure 5.25.

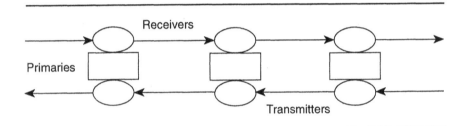

Figure 5.25.   Queued subprocesses message propagation.

```
/*ASYNCH1-X.C*/
#include    "[edward.ipc]ipc.inc"
#include    <stdlib.h>
#include    <stdio.h>

int AST_XMIT(io_statblk *write_status)
{
    printf("ASYNCH1 AST Post Transmit\n");
}
int AST_RCV(io_statblk *write_status)
{
    printf("ASYNCH1 AST Post Receive\n");
}

main()
{
    buffer      outtext, intext;
    short       channel;
    int         AST_PROC();
    char        task_id[] = "NODE01::\"TASK = ASYNCH2-x.COM\"";

    printf("ASYNCH1-x : Establishing Link to ASYNCH2-x\n");
```

```
if(!EstablishChannel(task_id, &channel))
{
    printf("ASYNCH1-x LINK : Unable to Establish Link\n");
}

strcpy(outtext,"Hello to ASYNCH2-x from ASYNCH1-x");
for(;;)
{
    printf("ASYNCH1 to ASYNCH2 - HELLO THIS IS A TEST\n");
    if(!TransmitMessage(channel, outtext, AST_XMIT))
    {
        printf("ASYNCH1-x TRANSMIT : Unable to Transmit via Channel\n");
    }

    if(!ReceiveMessage(channel, intext, AST_RCV))
    {
        printf("ASYNCH1-x RECEIVE : Unable to Receive via Channel\n");
    }
    printf("ASYNCH2-x to ASYNCH1-x %s\n",intext);

};
}
```

```
/*ASYNCH2-X.C*/
#include    "[edward.ipc]ipc.inc"

int AST_XMIT(io_statblk *write_status)
{
        printf("ASYNCH2 AST Post Transmit\n");

}
int AST_RCV(io_statblk *write_status)
{
        printf("ASYNCH2 AST Post Receive\n");

}

main()
{
        buffer        outtext, intext;
        short         channel;
        int           AST_PROC();
        char          task_id[] = "SYS$NET";
        FILE          logfile = fopen("ASYNCH2-x.LOG", "w+");

        if(!EstablishChannel(task_id,&channel))
```

```c
    {
        fprintf(logfile,"ASYNCH2-x LINK : Unable to Establish Link\n");
    }
    for(;;)
    {
        if(!ReceiveMessage(channel, intext, NULL))
        {
            fprintf(logfile,
                "ASYNCH2-x RECEIVE : Unable to Receive via Channel\n");
        }
        sprintf(outtext,"%s / Back to ya from ASYCNH2-x",intext);
        if(!TransmitMessage(channel, outtext, AST_XMIT))
        {
            fprintf(logfile,
                "ASYNCH2-x TRANSMIT : Unable to Transmit via Channel\n");
        }
    }
    fprintf(logfile,"\n ASYNCH2-x Complete \n");
    fclose(logfile);
}
```

6

Multicasting

Multicasting is a method of interprocess communications that operates using a method known as connectionless communications. This method operates exactly as its category implies—there exist no connections, or logical links, between processes. Essentially, this method allows a process to build and submit information to the network and have one or more nodes accept the information and forward it to the receive process. This capability is possible because of the flexibility of the DNA layers at each node. The functions available to perform multicast communications (MCAST) allow processes to connect to the lower layers of DNA and create a packet for submission as a frame to the network.

As an example, let's look at a simple client/server type of application. In MCAST, the system may be designed in such a way that provides one server, which manages a database, and any number of client applications requesting information from the server. As can be seen in Figure 6.1, the server process maintains a registered multicast address of AB-00-00-04-00-00 and the user protocol 0x0660. Whenever a client wishes to make a request from the server, a packet is built with the server's respective destination address, protocol, and the request. Once the respective node receives the packet and determines that the frame has the destination multicast address and protocol of the server, the information is passed to the server process. When the server is ready to respond, it prepares a packet with the clients' multicast address and protocol. The clients with the multicast address and protocol then receive and process the information accordingly.

From Figure 6.1 several different ideas should be noted. The first important note is that there are two client processes registered per multicast address and all related processes use the user protocol 0x0660. The important thing is that whenever a frame with a destination address of AB-00-00-04-00-01 and respective protocol is submitted to the network, all registered processes will accept that frame. This introduces an interesting idea regarding the development of distributed systems. What can also be seen here is that all processes are connected to the network instead of logically linked to each other. This may

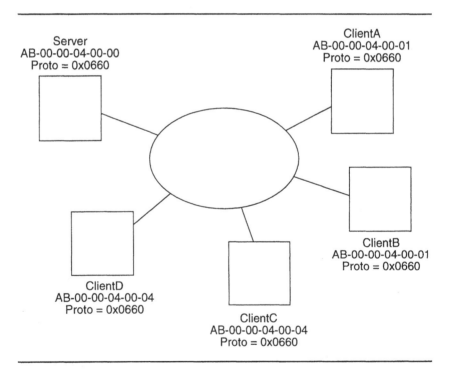

Figure 6.1.   Multicast configuration.

seem superfluous, but the processes do not maintain any form of direct connection but instead communicate over a common device—the network. This configuration also demonstrates an ability to allow ClientA to communicate with ClientC if desired. So far as flexibility is concerned, this configuration allows for the ability to attach any number of clients, provided the network can handle the additional utilization, in order to expand the system easily. As was explained in TIPC, channels, or logical links, were required between the processes and they had to be constantly monitored. In MCAST, the clients are not known until they make a request or, if anonymity is not desired, the client may send a hello message on startup.

PHASES OF MCAST

This implementation of interprocess communications is one of those areas that may be difficult to grasp at the beginning because there are no legitimate links between processes and there are no set methodologies required to perform MCAST. Instead, processes communicate by simply placing a packet on the network and having any registered node/object on the network intercept the packet for processing as required. This section will outline the phases involved in MCAST in a simple and straightforward manner. In order to assist in the explanation, periodic comparisons will be made to TIPC in order to show the similarities as well as the differences. While the phases explained here seem fairly concrete, variations may be made that allow for a broader application base. The one idea to keep in mind is that the limitations and strict design work placed on applications under TIPC may be curtailed and in some circumstances eliminated under MCAST.

One important fact to remember is that a process on, for instance, NODE01 cannot use multicasting to talk to another process on the same node. Recall that under TIPC this was possible because a logical link was simply routed back around to the process on that node through the DNA of that node. Under MCAST, the transmitting process connects below the primary layers of DNA responsible for establishing the respective logical links to another process. This means that, as frames are being transmitted, the transmitting node cannot receive frames at the same time over the same physical device. This leads to the point that a frame sent to another process on the same node must use a higher level of communications such as TIPC or similar methods.

MCAST Initiation

Before MCAST can be accomplished, the process must connect to the node's Ethernet device. This connection establishes a channel that is used for information transfer between the process and the device. The format for the task specification string in this case is simply the name of the device on the local node. See Table 6.1.

Once the channel to a controller has been returned from the System Service call, the controller's mode must then be set based on the desired operation to be performed. During this setup, a series of parameters are passed to the controller in order to define the protocol, size of the I/O buffers, multicast mode state, promiscuous mode state, and multicast address, as well as a plethora of other functions that can be performed with the controller. For additional information as to the available functions that can be defined for the controller, refer to the *VMS I/O User's Reference Manual: Part II* and SYS$LIBRARY:LIB.REQ.

MCAST Transmission

In TIPC it was stated that transmission of data from one process to another occurs over a logical link between the respective processes. Under MCAST, the channel is only available between a process and the controller. Once the information is passed out of the process along the channel for transmission, the controller

Table 6.1. Device/controller names.

XEA0:	DEUNA and DELUA
XQA0:	DEQNA and DELQA
ETA0:	DEBNA
ESA0:	DESVA

performs standard transmission procedures and submits the packet to the network as a frame. In such a situation, a transmit process and a receive process do not have to cooperate in order to have information transferred across the network. A majority of the work is accomplished by the device connected to the channel of the process.

MCAST Reception

Once a node receives the frame, the physical layer passes the frame up to the data link layer. The DNA layers then perform the standard address comparisons to see if that frame is destined for the node. If a module exists within that node that accepts the protocol and destination address of the respective packet, whether it be multicast or explicit, the information is passed up to that module, or process, for processing. If no respective module exists, the frame is not used.

MCAST Termination

In order to terminate an MCAST process, the process may issue a shutdown message to the controller over the channel. Once the call returns, the process should then simply deassign the channel. Recall that in TIPC the primary process and the process located at the other end of the channel should cooperate in the termination; however, since the channel is connected to a device, the device handles its own deassignment with the process on the channel. One question could be raised about notification of processes on other nodes that communicate with the process terminating the channel. This notification function depends on the paradigm utilized and will be discussed later.

IMPLEMENTATION

The following MCAST implementation takes into account the information previously discussed and incorporates actual code to assist in the explanation. This code has been implemented as part of a sample application for a client/server implementation. The idea behind this application was to send a record name from a client to a server and have the server return the information for that record back to the client for display. While reading the following description, the terms client and server are provided for explanation purposes in order to allow a simple means of understanding the concepts for this section. Later in this chapter, different paradigms will be made available for representation of other possible implementations of MCAST. As stated, code segments will be provided for explanation purposes; however, the complete source code for the client and server used in the examples is provided at the end of this chapter. It may be helpful to refer to this code as well during the explanations in order to assist in understanding the operation as a whole.

MCAST Client

An MCAST client is a process that communicates with one or more server processes or with other clients. One purpose of a client is to provide an interface in a distributed system in order to share resources. The user may be a person, a process, or any other user-type implementation that requires access to common network resources maintained by the server.

As can be seen in Figure 6.2, the client definitions maintain calls that are to be utilized in a structure sent to the controller on startup. One new include file is introduced, named IODEF.H, which maintains the IO$ declarations used during calls to the controller device during startup, transmit, receive, and shutdown. For a complete listing of all of the defines and macros available for these particular implementations, refer to the file SYS$LIBRARY:LIB.REQ and the *VMS I/O User's Reference Manual Part I* and *Part II*.

Figure 6.3 contains the extended characteristics buffer that is utilized in the controller() function of the client. This structure is passed to the controller on startup to notify the device of its required operating characteristics for the channel attached to the process. Note that the characteristics are not shared with other processes/channels and only affect that one channel's characteristics for the process. The buffer is to notify the device that it should preallocate 2 (_BFN) 1500-byte (_BUS) receive buffers where the default is normally 1. This parameter is used

```c
#include <descrip.h>                        /* String descriptor types          */
#include <stdio.h>                          /* Standard Input Output header     */
#include <iodef.h>                          /* Input Output definitions         */
#include <string.h>
#include <stdlib.h>

/* Extracted from SYS$LIBRARY:LIB.REQ */
#define NMA$C_PCLI_PTY 2830                  /* Protocol identifier              */
#define NMA$C_PCLI_PRM 2840                  /* Promiscuous mode identifier      */
#define NMA$C_PCLI_BFN 1105                  /* Receive buffer allocation identifier */
#define NMA$C_PCLI_BUS 2801                  /* Respective rcv buffer size       */
#define NMA$C_PCLI_PHA 2820                  /* Port address                     */
#define NMA$C_PCLI_PAD 2842                  /* Frame padding identifier         */
#define NMA$C_PCLI_FMT 2770                  /* Frame format                     */
#define NMA$C_PCLI_MLT 2841                  /* Multicast mode identifier        */
#define NMA$C_PCLI_MCA 2831                  /* Multicast address definition     */

#define NMA$C_STATE_ON 0                     /* State mode enabled               */
#define NMA$C_STATE_OFF 1                    /* State mode disabled              */

#define NMA$C_LINMC_SET 1                    /* Set multicast address            */
#define NMA$C_LINMC_CLR 2                    /* Clear the multicast addresses    */
#define NMA$C_LINMC_CAL 3                    /* Clear all multicast addresses    */

#define NMA$C_LINFM_ETH 1                    /* Ethernet format                  */

int status;
short channel;
short iosb[4];
unsigned char buffer[1500];
```

Figure 6.2.   Client process defines.

109

```
StartupBuffer =
{
    NMA$C_PCLI_BFN, 2,                              /* Setup 2 receive buffers       */
    NMA$C_PCLI_PTY, 0x0660,                         /* Register for user protocol    */
    NMA$C_PCLI_BUS, 1500,                           /* 1500 byte receive buffer      */
    NMA$C_PCLI_PAD, NMA$C_STATE_OFF,                /* Frame padding disabled        */
    NMA$C_PCLI_PRM, NMA$C_STATE_OFF,                /* Promiscuous disabled          */
    NMA$C_PCLI_FMT, NMA$C_LINFM_ETH,                /* Ethernet frame format         */
    NMA$C_PCLI_MLT, NMA$C_STATE_OFF,                /* Multicast mode off            */
    NMA$C_PCLI_MCA,                                 /* Filter multicast address      */
    (short)sizeof(short)+6,                         /* Size of counted string        */
    (short)NMA$C_LINMC_SET,                         /* Set the address               */
    0xab,0x00,0x00,0x04,0x00,0x01                   /* Multicast address             */
};
```

Figure 6.3.   Extended characteristics buffer for startup.

to notify the device that it should maintain at least two frames when the process connected to the channel has no read requests queued to the device. Notice also that the padding (_PAD) of the Ethernet packet (_FMT) is disabled, which, as previously stated, allows for data to range from 46 to 1500 bytes with padding performed within the data portion of the frame. The remainder of the buffer maintains information used to register the process with a multicast address, specific protocol, and promiscuous mode state at the data link layer.

As can be seen, the respective process is registered to receive protocol 0x0660 (_PTY) with a multicast address of AB-00-00-04-00-01 (_MCA). The multicast address parameter maintains a counted string buffer where the first parameter maintains the count of bytes available in the string and the second parameter may be _SET to set one or more multicast addresses, _CLR to clear an address, or _CAL to clear all multicast addresses. The remaining elements of the parameter maintain the 6-byte multicast addresses to set or clear depending on the previous state parameter.

Note here the states of the promiscuous mode (_PRM) and multicast mode (_MLT) parameters. The state of these parameters depends on the implementation. For this implementation, multicast and promiscuous modes disabled, the process will receive only those packets with a protocol of 0x0660 and the stated destination multicast address of AB-00- 00-04-00-01. If multicast is enabled, all multicast addresses will be accepted. If promiscuous mode is enabled, any and all packets will be accepted without regard to the protocol and multicast address registered for the process.

Notice in Figure 6.4 that an operation exists that loops through a series of calls to SYS$ASSIGN in an attempt to attach to the device defined in the descriptor and create a channel. Once the channel is created, it is used in a call to SYS$QIOW in order to set up and start the controller for the respective channel. During the call to SYS$QIOW, the extended characteristics buffer is passed in P2 with functions for IO$_SETMODE and IO$M_STARTUP, which tells the device to start up with the modes specified in P2.

Once the controller is set up, the rest of the functions operate in a manner similar to that of TIPC and every other implementation to be introduced. As can be seen in Figure 6.5, two buffers

```c
struct dsc$descriptor_s devicedescriptor =        /* Device name descriptor       */
                   { 0, DSC$K_DTYPE_T, DSC$K_CLASS_S, 0};

                                    /* Assign the respective device    */
for (i=0, status = 0; (status != 1) && (device[i][0] != '*') ; i++)
{
        devicedescriptor.dsc$a_pointer = device[i];
        devicedescriptor.dsc$w_length = strlen(device[i]);
        status = sys$assign(&devicedescriptor, &channel, 0, 0);


}

if (!(status & 1)) lib$stop(status);
        printf("Controller %s\n",device[i-1]);

                                    /* Start the controller            */
status = sys$qiow(0, channel, IO$_SETMODE + IO$M_STARTUP + IO$M_CTRL,
                  iosb, 0, 0, &StartupBufferDescriptor, 0, 0, 0, 0);
```

Figure 6.4. Controller startup.

are created for the transmission where one contains the required destination address and protocol and the other contains the data to transfer. In the figure, XMTP5 contains the respective destination multicast address in the first 6 bytes while the last 2 bytes contain the protocol. The protocol value is reversed from the previous declarations (i.e., 0x0660 → 6006) in the extended characteristics buffer. This information is utilized in assigning the information to the outgoing frame's fields for proper routing of the information through the network.

The XMTBUF buffer allows the storage of up to 14 bytes for transmission to the said destination. This buffer was set up for demonstration only and may be extended to the largest data field size of the frame depending on the state of the padding (_PAD) parameter. The following memcpy() function simply takes information and copies it over to the transmit buffer for transmission to the remote node. Now that the buffers are prepared and the data is ready for transmission, the SYS$QIOW function is utilized to transfer the information from the process, down the channel to the device. In the call to SYS$QIOW, the buffers are passed to the function as well as the channel to the device and the function IO$_WRITELBLK. The device then prepares the information into a legitimate frame and submits it to the physical layer for transmission on the network.

In order to receive information from the device, the SYS$QIOW function is called with the IO$_READLBLK func-

```
char xmtp5[8] = {0xab,0x00,0x00,0x04,0x01,0x02,0x60,0x06};
char xmtbuf[14]= {0x00,0x00,0x00,0x00,0x00,0x00,0x00,0x00,
                  0x00,0x00,0x00,0x00,0x00,0x00};

printf("SENDING\n");

memcpy(xmtbuf,xmitinfo,13);
                          /*Write using a Wait                   */
status = sys$qiow(0, channel, IO$_WRITELBLK, iosb, 0, 0,
                  &xmtbuf[0], sizeof(xmtbuf), 0, 0, &xmtp5[0], 0);
```

Figure 6.5.   Transmission.

```
status = sys$qiow(0, channel, IO$_READLBLK, iosb, 0, 0,
      &buffer[14], sizeof(buffer)-14, 0, 0, &buffer[0], 0);

printf("DATA : %s\n",&buffer[14]);
memcpy(descr,&buffer[14],24);
descr[24]='\0';
```

Figure 6.6.   Reception.

tion. The received information is then placed into a set of buffers for utilization of the information within the process. As can be seen in Figure 6.6, the P1 buffer of the SYS$QIOW call receives the data field of the frame. P2 maintains the size of the information required to be retrieved and placed into the respective buffer of P1. P5 maintains a buffer to capture the header of the frame, specifically the source and destination address as well as the protocol of the frame.

MCAST Server

An MCAST server is a process that services requests from clients. In a connectionless environment such as MCAST, client/ server implementations are easier to implement because they provide a means of directing frames without direct connection. This adds flexibility to the server in that it may service any client that requests on a first come, first serve basis—essentially unsolicited requests. Recall that under TIPC, the channels were polled, whereas under MCAST, frames are simply created and sent so that the clients may intercept that frame and process it accordingly.

The definitions for the server for this implementation are identical to the client's definitions as depicted in Figure 6.2. The other characteristic of the server similar to the client is that of the controller() function utilized to start up the controller on the channel. In Figure 6.7, it should be noted that the only difference is in the multicast address definitions.

In this instance, two multicast addresses are defined for the

```
StartupBuffer =
{
                        /* Setup 2 receive buffers      */
     NMA$C_PCLI_BFN, 2,
                        /* Register for user protocol    */
     NMA$C_PCLI_PTY, 0x0660,
                        /* 1500 byte receive buffer      */
     NMA$C_PCLI_BUS, 1500,
                        /* Frame padding disabled        */
     NMA$C_PCLI_PAD, NMA$C_STATE_OFF,
                        /* Promiscuous mode disabled     */
     NMA$C_PCLI_PRM, NMA$C_STATE_OFF,
                        /* Ethernet frame format         */
     NMA$C_PCLI_FMT, NMA$C_LINFM_ETH,
                        /* Multicast mode off            */
     NMA$C_PCLI_MLT, NMA$C_STATE_OFF,
                        /* Filter multicast address      */
     NMA$C_PCLI_MCA,
                        /* Size of counted string        */
          (short)sizeof(short)+12,
                        /* Set the address               */
          (short)NMA$C_LINMC_SET,
                        /* Multicast address1 for server */
          0xab,0x00,0x00,0x04,0x01,0x01,
                        /* Multicast address2 for server */
          0xab,0x00,0x00,0x04,0x01,0x02
};
```

Figure 6.7.   Controller startup.

server. This operation is only for demonstration purposes and is presented to show that multiple multicast addresses may be defined per process whether the process be a server or a client. As can be seen, the process is registered to receive protocol 0x0660 (_PTY) with multicast addresses of AB-00-00-04-01-01 and AB-00-00-04-01-02 (_MCA). As previously stated, the multicast address parameter is a counted string. Notice that the first parameter now contains 14 bytes, instead of 8 for the client, in order to maintain the additional 6 bytes for the second address. This application of multicast addresses allows two multicast ad-

```
char  xmtp5[8] = {0xab,0x00,0x00,0x04,0x00,0x01,0x60,0x06};
char  xmtbuf[14] = {0x00,0x00,0x00,0x00,0x00,0x00,0x00,0x00,
                    0x00,0x00,0x00,0x00,0x00,0x00};

printf("SENDING\n");

memcpy(xmtbuf,xmitinfo,13);
                             /*Write using a Wait              */
status = sys$qiow(0, channel, IO$_WRITELBLK, iosb, 0, 0,
         &xmtbuf[0], sizeof(xmtbuf), 0, 0, &xmtp5[0], 0);
```

Figure 6.8.   Transmission.

dresses to be accepted by the server so long as the protocol is
0x0660. To correlate the addresses between the client and the
server, Figure 6.5's XMTP5 buffer contains one of the multicast
addresses registered by the server in the extended characteristics buffer of Figure 6.7.

The startup call to SYS$ASSIGN and SYS$QIOW are identical between the server and client processes. The only negligible
difference with the startup operation between the two processes
is that of the second multicast address; however, that was added
for demonstration purposes only and does not mean that the second address is a requirement for operation.

In Figure 6.8, transmission is accomplished in a manner similar
to the method used in the client except for the XMTP5 buffer. Recall
in the client that the multicast destination address for transmission
was AB-00-00-04-01-02. In the server, the destination multicast
address for transmission is now AB-00-00-04-00-01 in order to send
a frame out to the multicast addresses registered to the clients.

The receive operation of the server is exactly as that used in
the client. All calls to the SYS$QIO System Service function
maintain the same buffers and operation as utilized in the client receive-oriented function.

MCAST Output

Now that the source code has been reviewed for the client and
server tasks, let's review the output of the processes and see

Table 6.2.   Sample output.

CLIENT Output	SERVER Output
Controller ESA0: QIO Status: 1	Controller ESA0: QIO Status: 1
SENDING RECEIVING Checking DATA: RECORD 1248 VALUE DESCR: RECORD 1248 VALUE	RECEIVING Checking DATA: REC1248VAL SENDING
SENDING RECEIVING Checking DATA: RECORD 1249 VALUE DESCR: RECORD 1249 VALUE	RECEIVING Checking DATA: REC1249VAL SENDING
SENDING RECEIVING Checking DATA: RECORD 1250 VALUE DESCR: RECORD 1250 VALUE	RECEIVING Checking DATA: REC1250VAL SENDING

what happens during each step. As can be seen in Table 6.2, the
first step is to connect a channel to the controller and, not shown,
start up and set the mode of the controller. The next step is to
issue a transmit of the record name from the client to the server.
This step is seen as SENDING in the client column. The server
then states RECEIVING/Checking to signify that it has received
the client's record name request. The client then states RECEIV-
ING/Checking in order to signify the reception of the data from
the server. The client then prints the output of the data from the
server in two places, signified as DATA and DESCR, in order to
display the received data.

PARADIGMS

Since the basic understanding of one MCAST implementation
has been presented, let's look at a few different paradigms in
which MCAST may be utilized. In order to follow with the set

methods of the book, a client/server and a peer-to-peer method will be presented. Since these sample implementations will be utilized throughout the remainder of the book for consistency, the different views will provide the reader with many options to develop legitimate applications using the methods presented.

Peer-to-Peer

A peer-to-peer implementation, as designed around MCAST, involves, as before, independent processes on separate nodes that occasionally perform health checks with each other to determine the states of the respective nodes/systems. Regarding a distributed system, using MCAST makes distributed implementations much easier and more straightforward than other process communication paradigms. This is because of the connectionless characteristic of the system making each process independent and parallel but still in contact with the other processes of the system for information transfer and management across the system.

As can be seen in Figure 6.9, there exist four independent systems that perform the same function but operate as redundant backups to each other. Of course, in order to maintain a

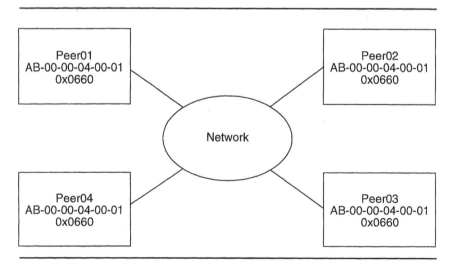

Figure 6.9.   Peer-to-peer configuration.

backup scheme such as this, all nodes must receive and process the information; however, only one node can respond based on the result of the processing. Processing incoming information is very straightforward. As was seen in Figure 6.3, all four nodes maintain the same multicast address (00-01). When information is destined for an information processor, all four nodes will accept the information (based on protocol and multicast address). Once the information has been processed, a result, based on the specific information, must be sent out onto the network. If all four nodes transmitted simultaneously, there would obviously be wasted network utilization, not to mention the confusion at the destination node of the outgoing frame.

Periodically, health checks are performed between the processes. In order to submit this health check properly, each node must perform the check to determine which nodes are active information processors. Let's assume that Peer01 is initially the primary processor. On occasion, each node will send out a hello request message in a frame destined for multicast address 00-01. Remember that even though the transmitting node has the multicast address, it will not intercept the packet that it is transmitting. Once this frame is received by the other three nodes, these nodes respond to Peer01 with an acknowledgment frame. Once Peer01 receives the frames, the source addresses are registered in a database in order to maintain a means of knowing the states of all peers during each hello poll. If at any time a node should either respond with a negative status or not respond to a hello poll, that node will be assumed to be inactive. At that instant, if the inactive node was the primary processor, the next node in the hierarchy of redundant backups will assume the responsibility of the primary processor. In this instance, Peer02 would become primary processor.

Client/Server

A client/server (monitor) implementation is quite simple to implement using MCAST. Recall that such a paradigm involves a centralized data server that is interrogated by a series of client processes for information management purposes. Recall as well that under TIPC, a direct logical link was required between the clients and the server as well as a means of channel, or link, management within the server.

With MCAST, clients may come and go as they please without having to rely directly on the server process. Recall that under TIPC, it was the responsibility of the server process to initialize the clients; however, under MCAST, clients initialize themselves but may take on a couple of different means of initializing communication with the server. Several different methods may be utilized depending on the implementation; however, the underlying communication implementation will remain essentially the same regardless of the paradigm utilized.

Passive servers. Passive servers, or monitors, only provide information as a result of a request from a client. In such a situation, a server is idle unless a request has arrived from a client. Situations that require such a scenario do not require data to constantly be sent to the clients and are usually implemented in the realm of static user interfaces. An example of a passive server is a data management system utilized in, for instance, a real estate office where a realtor would require information on all 2-bedroom, 2-bath homes in a certain area. Since the information is not truly time-critical, the information to the user does not have to be updated every couple of seconds. The information only needs to be sent to the user when requested.

Active servers. Active servers provide a means of servicing requests from clients as well as providing information to clients as the information becomes available. Under certain circumstances it becomes necessary to have a server service requests from clients and also issue information to all, or certain, clients as required from the server's point of view. The most applicable areas for active servers are applications which require up-to-the-second information for devices that are being controlled and monitored remotely. If a user is watching incoming information for a device in the field, the user would obviously want to see the information as it changes for the field device. The server would accept the information, process it accordingly, and send it out onto the network. All user processes, or clients, that require a particular piece of information will intercept the frame and issue it for update to the user's display.

Client aware. Client-aware implementations take into account the fact that the server is aware of all currently available clients. This type of implementation is created by having a series of clients that send a hello message to the server(s) when they are initialized. This type of scenario is useful in a distributed processing environment where processing is truly distributed on several different nodes. Let's take a look at a centralized server example that interacts with a series of devices located in the field for controlling and monitoring the states of the devices. The central server would collect information from the field devices and transfer this data to certain clients for processing purposes.

As can be seen in Figure 6.10, the server would act as a traffic cop to send the correct information to the client that is to process the respective information. When a client becomes active, or is initialized, it would send a message to the server's multicast address stating that it is responsible for temperature measurement

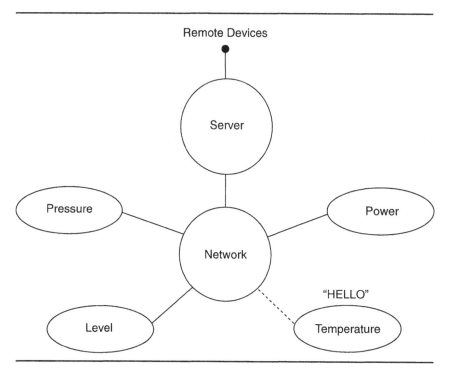

Figure 6.10.   Client-aware scenario.

processing and management. The server would register the client's information in a local database for routing purposes. The clients would be a series of processes that process information based on their respective characteristics (i.e., Pressure, Power consumption, etc.). The idea behind this type of implementation would be to provide a distributed processing situation where different nodes would be responsible for different data types. In such a situation, the server would request and update the information for the independent clients as well as maintain an interface to the remote devices. This is, of course, an example but would operate well in an environment where several thousand remote devices must be monitored. Such a situation would take a tremendous amount of horsepower for one processor, but if the processing was distributed across several nodes the operation of the processors would logically be more efficient.

Anonymous client. Anonymous client implementations involve a server that is not actually concerned about the clients available on the system. In such a situation, the clients would initiate any and all data transfers between the client and the server. As can be seen in Figure 6.11, the server is no longer the center of the operation but is instead acting as a reference for the clients.

In such a situation, Client01 would operate as normal until a request is sent to the server. The server then receives the MCAST frame, processes the information accordingly, and responds. If no requests are received by the server, by function, the server goes into a wait state.

Overview. A complete overview of a sample client/server implementation is in order to take the information just provided and consolidate it into a legitimate system. As can be seen in Figure 6.12, each client in the example is the front end for a user interface that maintains data for viewing by a user. Each client maintains a unique multicast address (01-0X) and a group multicast address (00-02). The unique addresses are utilized in order to allow the server to communicate with a specific client and to allow one client to communicate with another—a private phone line. The server process maintains a multicast address of 00-01 to allow access to the server and not interfere with the clients by

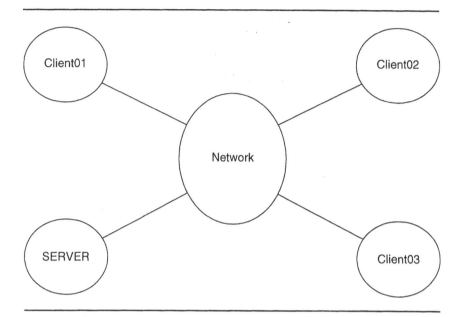

Figure 6.11. Anonymous client scenario.

having them intercept a frame destined for the server. Assume that the server is an active server implemented in the client-aware scenario.

With respect to the active server scenario, the server submits information to the multicast address 00-02 to be processed and intercepted by all client processes. This information may consist of synchronization information and general systemwide operating parameters. Assume that at a particular instant the server receives information from the field that is directly associated with a device located at Plant 1. The server locates the multicast address for the process from the client-aware database associated with Plant 1, Client01, and transfers the information via MCAST to the destination user interface for Plant 1. This type of operation is also performed for Plant 2 and 3 information from the field devices to the user interface.

On certain occasions, the user will need to request certain information from the server. In these circumstances the client will submit a request to the server for information regarding the

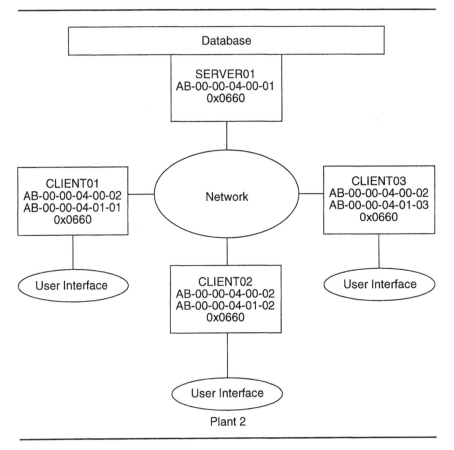

Figure 6.12. Client/server multicast example.

respective plant. The client formats the information and submits it to the network with a destination multicast address of 00-01 for the server. The server receives the frame and may perform three response-oriented actions. First, the server may issue a response back to the client based on the source address located in the source address of the previously received request frame. Second, the server may respond to the client's multicast address based on the Plant number-related information that is associated back to the respective client. The plant-related information was collected during the initial hello message relating to the client-aware scenario. The final situation involves responding to all clients by way of the client group multicast address of 00-02.

One additional note to make here is a reason for the use of MCAST in the client/server scenario. In such a situation there may exist the standard client/server paradigm combined with peer-to-peer implementation. This type of implementation allows for redundant backups for the clients and the server. As can be seen in Figure 6.13, two clients are available for Plant 1 and operate in a parallel manner since both processes maintain the same multicast addresses. If at any time one of the clients should drop out, the other would continue operating; however, if peer-to-peer implementation is utilized, each process would be aware of the other process's status in order to properly maintain orderly I/O with the server.

DEVELOPMENT

Developing an MCAST implementation does not involve the same stringent requirements as is required under TIPC. The primary advantage to using a connectionless communication environment is that of flexibility. The one problem involved in the development of an MCAST implementation is that there is a whole new set of situations to be aware of for such an implementation. This section

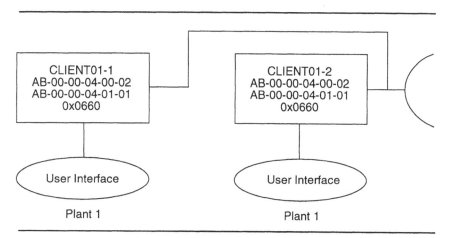

Figure 6.13.   Redundant MCAST clients.

will review only a few of the situations that will be relevant for active and passive servers regarding communication maintenance, message processing, and channel contention.

Active/Passive Servers

Active and passive server uses vary between implementations. Implementing an active server for a simple data management facility would possibly be overkill and would bog down the network, while a passive server in a control center would definitely cause user response problems. The final decision is left up to the implementation requirements as well as the developer.

Communication Maintenance

One problem involved with connectionless communications is the possibility of missing incoming frames that may be destined for that process. Recall under TIPC when the processes did not cooperate in the transfer by issuing a read on one side of the channel when a write was issued at the other end. The message was not lost; however, no message was transferred. Under MCAST, operating at a lower level, frames will still be transmitted if the receiving process is not ready to receive the information; however, the message may be lost.

One solution to this situation is to implement an intermediate buffer, which operates as a temporary storage in the operation of high-speed data transfer. As can be seen in Figure 6.14, there exist two network processes to manage incoming and outgoing information, respectively. Attached to both processes are buffers, which are used to maintain the information before it is sent and/or received. At the top of the structure is a process that is used to process the information as it appears in the incoming buffer and add information to the outgoing buffer for transmission.

As an example, assume that there exists a frame arriving at the node of the respective processes. The frame is received by the node allowing the information from the frame to be routed to the incoming network process. The information processor then reads that information from the buffer, processes it, and, if required,

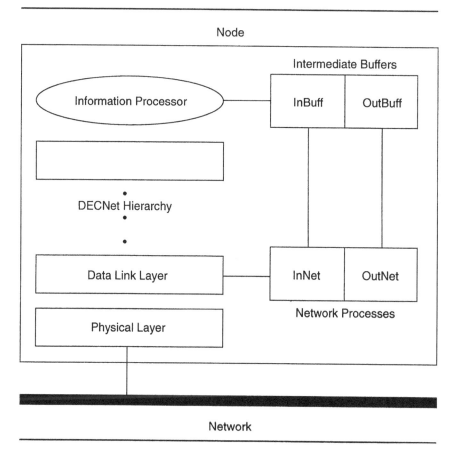

Node

Figure 6.14.   Intermediate buffers.

places information in the outgoing buffer for transmission by the
network write process. Obviously, a one-frame scenario would ren-
der this implementation overkill. Assume instead that several
hundred packets per second arrive at the node. As these frames
arrive, the information can be buffered in the incoming buffer until the information processor is ready for them. The flip side to
using this scenario is that of missing packets. Assume again that
several hundred packets arrive at the node without the intermediate buffers. Once the information processor receives information
to process, it may miss subsequent frames while processing the

received frame until it issues another read request to accept the next frame's information from the device.

A second means of communication management is through synchronization between communication processes. This method is quite simple in that all cooperating processes rely on a DataServerReady message to be sent out onto the network, which, in response, allows one client to submit an Acknowledge and a data frame to the server. This method requires a bit more contemplation in order to properly manage handshaking between the clients and the server(s).

As can be seen in Figure 6.15, the server process sends out a message to all clients that the server is ready to receive more data. Once all clients receive the message, each client will attempt to submit an Acknowledge to all clients and the server in order to gain control of the system. Once a client does submit an Acknowledge to the network, all other clients wait until the next time the server submits a Ready message. The client currently having control over the system sends its data to the server for processing. This operation is continuously repeated throughout the lifetime of the system. In a situation where no clients have

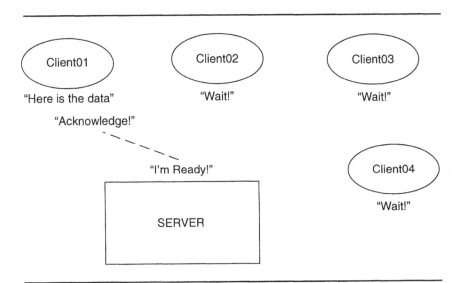

Figure 6.15. Handshake communication.

data, none of the clients will respond, which will place all clients in a position to gain control of the system whenever they are ready to transmit.

Message Processing

With MCAST, a simple and flexible means of being able to transfer many different structures across the network is available; however, a means of determining how to process the information is required. Under most circumstances the receive process can select a process direction based on the protocol; however, certain circumstances will arise that will require several different structures for one process. If such a multi-message process should exist, a means must be provided to determine how to segregate the structures for that one process.

Single message. A single-message protocol-based message processor will maintain only one method for processing the incoming information. Such a situation lends itself to very straightforward development and implementation. Recall that a process may register itself as a specific protocol receiver. In such a situation, the process can maintain a specific processing algorithm that only operates on one specific structure. Let's say, for instance, that a single message processor processes only information for a particular database record type (i.e., customer addresses). The process does not have to prepare any special processing algorithm to determine how to handle the message since it knows that it can only receive and process that one message type. Once the frame is passed up to the process, a structure may simply be joined with the message to extract the information as required.

Multi message. In a multi-message protocol-based process, the process registers as a specific protocol-based receiver but may receive more than one message type. In such a situation a means of determining the message type is required in order to facilitate an appropriate processing procedure determination. As can be seen in Figure 6.16, a determinant is added to a buffer to allow the receiving process to determine which type of message is in the buffer. In Figure 6.17, the processing portion of the process

```
struct message
{
    int type;        /* Identifies the type of message */
    void *buffer;    /* Message      */
}
```

Figure 6.16.   Sample message structure.

```
int Process(struct message msg)
{
    switch(msg.type)
    {
        case 1:    {
                       /*code*/
                   }
        case 2:    {
                       /*code*/
                   }
    }
}
```

Figure 6.17.   Sample processing sequence.

will read the type of message that has arrived and will process the message in the buffer based on that type.

Channel Contention

One problem that had to be handled under TIPC was that of contention on the channel. Such a situation arose from the fact that two processes had to communicate over one channel. Under MCAST, the concern is now minimized because of the way that this type of communications is handled. Recall that the process is connected to the DNA hierarchy at the data link layer, which allows for more control over the handling of the frame transmissions and receptions. Recall as well that the data link layer modules, in cooperation with the physical layer, handles contention/collisions on the network. In such a situation the process is using the functions of the data link and physical layers in handling the problems involved with transmission and reception of information—frames.

SAMPLE CLIENT/SERVER APPLICATION

The following pages contain source code for three applications that can be utilized to test a small client/server implementation. The first two sets of code contain the source for client processes while the final set of code is the source for the server. The idea behind this implementation is to have a server operating on a central host that maintains a small database. The client processes start up and request a series of records from the server. The server receives the request, prints the output, then returns the requested information to the client. The client then prints the received information to the screen. Sample output for this implementation is given in Table 6.2.

Notice that the server process maintains two multicast addresses for itself. One of the clients makes requests to the first multicast address while the other client makes requests to the second address. This has no bearing on the actual operation of the application and will operate the same so long as the clients are adjusted accordingly. The purpose of this implementation is to demonstrate the ability of registering multiple multicast addresses for one process and to show the general operation of multicasting.

```c
/* CLIENT.C */
#include <descrip.h>        /*String descriptor types          */
#include <stdio.h>          /*Standard Input Output header      */
#include <iodef.h>          /*Input Output definitions          */
#include <string.h>
#include <stdlib.h>

/* Extracted from SYS$LIBRARY:LIB.REQ */
#define NMA$C_PCLI_PTY 2830     /* Protocol identifier                       */
#define NMA$C_PCLI_PRM 2840     /* Promiscuous mode identifier               */
#define NMA$C_PCLI_BFN 1105     /* Receive buffer allocation identifier      */
#define NMA$C_PCLI_BUS 2801     /* Respective rcv buffer size                */
#define NMA$C_PCLI_PHA 2820     /* Port address                              */
#define NMA$C_PCLI_PAD 2842     /* Frame padding identifier                  */
#define NMA$C_PCLI_FMT 2770     /* Frame format                              */
#define NMA$C_PCLI_MLT 2841     /* Multicast mode identifier                 */
#define NMA$C_PCLI_MCA 2831     /* Multicast address definition              */

#define NMA$C_STATE_ON  0       /* State mode enabled                        */
#define NMA$C_STATE_OFF 1       /* State mode disabled                       */

#define NMA$C_LINMC_SET 1       /* Set multicast address                     */
#define NMA$C_LINMC_CLR 2       /* Clear the multicast addresses             */
#define NMA$C_LINMC_CAL 3       /* Clear all multicast addresses             */

#define NMA$C_LINFM_ETH 1       /* Ethernet format                           */

int status;
short channel;
```

```c
short iosb[4];
unsigned char buffer[1500];

/*-------------------------------------------------------------
/* controller()
/*-------------------------------------------------------------
/* Open the ethernet controller.
/*-------------------------------------------------------------*/
void controller()
{
    char device[5][6] = {"XEA0:", "XQA0:", "ESA0:", "ETA0:", "*"};
    int i, status;

    struct
    {
        short   BFN;
        long    BFN_VAL;
        short   PTY;
        long    PTY_VAL;
        short   BUS;
        long    BUS_VAL;
        short   PAD;
        long    PAD_VAL;
        short   PRM;
        int     PRM_VAL;
        short   ETH;
        long    ETH_VAL;
        short   MLT;
        long    MLT_VAL;
        short   MADDR;
        short   MADDR_SIZEa;
```

```
        short   MADDR_CMDa;
        char    MADDR_VAL1a;
        char    MADDR_VAL2a;
        char    MADDR_VAL3a;
        char    MADDR_VAL4a;
        char    MADDR_VAL5a;
        char    MADDR_VAL6a;
} StartupBuffer =
{
                                        /* Setup 2 receive buffers    */
NMA$C_PCLI_BFN, 2,                      /* Register for user protocol */
NMA$C_PCLI_PTY, 0x0660,                 /* 1500 byte receive buffer   */
NMA$C_PCLI_BUS, 1500,                   /* Frame padding disabled     */
NMA$C_PCLI_PAD, NMA$C_STATE_OFF,        /* Promiscuous disabled       */
NMA$C_PCLI_PRM, NMA$C_STATE_OFF,        /* Ethernet frame format      */
NMA$C_PCLI_FMT, NMA$C_LINFM_ETH,        /* Multicast mode off         */
NMA$C_PCLI_MLT, NMA$C_STATE_OFF,        /* Filter multicast address   */
NMA$C_PCLI_MCA,                         /* Size of counted string     */
(short)sizeof(short)+6,                 /* Set the address            */
(short)NMA$C_LINMC_SET,                 /* Multicast address          */
```

```
                    0xab,0x00,0x00,0x04,0x00,0x01
    };

struct
{
    int size;
    int addr;
} StartupBufferDescriptor =
{
    sizeof(StartupBuffer),              /* Size and address of startup   */
    &StartupBuffer                      /* buffer                        */
};

                                        /* Device name descriptor        */
struct dsc$descriptor_s devicedescriptor =
                    { 0, DSC$K_DTYPE_T, DSC$K_CLASS_S, 0};

                                        /* Assign the respective device  */
for (i=0, status = 0; (status != 1) && (device[i][0] != '*') ; i++)
{
    devicedescriptor.dsc$a_pointer = device[i];
    devicedescriptor.dsc$w_length = strlen(device[i]);
    status = sys$assign(&devicedescriptor, &channel, 0, 0);
}

if (!(status & 1)) lib$stop(status);
    printf("Controller %s\n",device[i-1]);

                                        /* Start the controller          */
```

```c
    status = sys$qiow(0, channel, IO$_SETMODE + IO$M_STARTUP + IO$M_CTRL,
                      iosb, 0, 0, 0, &StartupBufferDescriptor, 0, 0, 0, 0);
    printf("QIO Status : %d\n",status);

    if (!(status & 1)) lib$stop(status);
    if ((iosb[0] & 1) != 1)
    {
        printf("STARTUP ERROR = %d %d %d\n",
               iosb[0], iosb[1], iosb[2], iosb[3]);
        printf("             = %2x %2x %2x %2x\n",
               iosb[0], iosb[1], iosb[2], iosb[3]);
        exit(iosb[0]);
    }
}

/*-------------------------------------------------------------*/
/* checkwriteether()                                           */
/*-------------------------------------------------------------*/
/* This function simply reads a packet matching the mcast adrs and protocol */
/*----------------------------------------------------------------------*/
int checkwriteether(char descr[27])
{
    int i;

    printf("RECEIVING\n");
    printf("Checking\n");

                                    /* Read and WAIT for a matching packet    */
```

```c
status = sys$qiow(0, channel, IO$_READLBLK, iosb, 0, 0,
                  &buffer[14], sizeof(buffer)-14, 0, 0, &buffer[0], 0);

printf("DATA : %s\n",&buffer[14]);
memcpy(descr,&buffer[14],24);
descr[24]='\0';

if (!(status & 1))
{
     lib$stop(status);
}

if (iosb[0] != 1)
{
     printf("ERROR = %2x %2x %2x %2x\n",
            iosb[0], iosb[1], iosb[2], iosb[3]);
     lib$stop(iosb[0]);
}

return iosb[1] + 14;              /* Return the number of bytes transferred       */
}
/*-------------------------------------------------------------------------------*/
/* writeether()                                                                  */
/*-------------------------------------------------------------------------------*/
/* This function writes a packet to the ethernet                                 */
/*-------------------------------------------------------------------------------*/
int writeether(char xmitinfo[13])
{
     int i;
                                  /* Server multicast addresses                   */
```

```c
char    xmtp5[8]    = {0xab,0x00,0x00,0x04,0x01,0x01,0x60,0x06};
char    xmtbuf[14]  = {0x00,0x00,0x00,0x00,0x00,0x00,0x00,0x00,
                       0x00,0x00,0x00,0x00,0x00,0x00};

printf("SENDING\n");

memcpy(xmtbuf,xmitinfo,13);                 /* Write using a Wait       */

status = sys$qiow(0, channel, IO$_WRITELBLK, iosb, 0, 0,
                  &xmtbuf[0], sizeof(xmtbuf), 0, 0, &xmtp5[0], 0);

if (!(status & 1))
{
    lib$stop(status);
}

if (iosb[0] != 1)
{
    printf("ERROR = %2x %2x %2x %2x\n",
           iosb[0], iosb[1], iosb[2], iosb[3]);
    lib$stop(iosb[0]);
}
return iosb[1] + 14;                         /* Return number of bytes transferred */
}

/*--------------------------------------------------------------------*/
/* main()
/*--------------------------------------------------------------------*/
main()
```

```
{
    char    descr[25];
    int i;
    char    recid[10][13] = {"REC1248VAL","REC1249VAL","REC1250VAL",
                             "REC1251VAL","REC1252VAL","REC1253VAL",
                             "REC1254VAL","REC1255VAL", "REC1257VAL"};

    controller();
    for (i=0;i<10;i++)
    {
        writeether(&recid[i][0]);
        checkwriteether(descr);
        printf("DESCR : %s\n",descr);
    }
}
```

```
/* CLIENT2.C */
#include <descrip.h>        /* String descriptor types          */
#include <stdio.h>          /* Standard Input Output header      */
#include <iodef.h>          /* Input Output definitions          */
#include <string.h>
#include <stdlib.h>

/* Extracted from SYS$LIBRARY:LIB.REQ */
#define NMA$C_PCLI_PTY 2830           /* Protocol identifier       */
```

```c
#define NMA$C_PCLI_PRM 2840          /* Promiscuous mode identifier          */
#define NMA$C_PCLI_BFN 1105          /* Receive buffer allocation identifier */
#define NMA$C_PCLI_BUS 2801          /* Respective rcv buffer size           */
#define NMA$C_PCLI_PHA 2820          /* Port address                         */
#define NMA$C_PCLI_PAD 2842          /* Frame padding identifier             */
#define NMA$C_PCLI_FMT 2770          /* Frame format                         */
#define NMA$C_PCLI_MLT 2841          /* Multicast mode identifier            */
#define NMA$C_PCLI_MCA 2831          /* Multicast address definition         */

#define NMA$C_STATE_ON 0             /* State mode enabled                   */
#define NMA$C_STATE_OFF 1            /* State mode disabled                  */

#define NMA$C_LINMC_SET 1            /* Set multicast address                */
#define NMA$C_LINMC_CLR 2            /* Clear the multicast addresses        */
#define NMA$C_LINMC_CAL 3            /* Clear all multicast addresses        */

#define NMA$C_LINFM_ETH 1            /* Ethernet format                      */

int status;
short channel;
short iosb[4];
unsigned char buffer[1500];

/*-----------------------------------------------------------------------
/* controller()
/*-----------------------------------------------------------------------
/* Open the ethernet controller.
/*-----------------------------------------------------------------------*/
void controller()
{
```

```c
        char device[5][6] = {"XEA0:", "XQA0:", "ESA0:", "ETA0:", "*"};
        int i, status;
struct
{
        short   BFN;
        long    BFN_VAL;
        short   PTY;
        long    PTY_VAL;
        short   BUS;
        long    BUS_VAL;
        short   PAD;
        long    PAD_VAL;
        short   PRM;
        int     PRM_VAL;
        short   ETH;
        long    ETH_VAL;
        short   MLT;
        long    MLT_VAL;
        short   MADDR;
        short   MADDR_SIZEa;
        short   MADDR_CMDa;
        char    MADDR_VAL1a;
        char    MADDR_VAL2a;
        char    MADDR_VAL3a;
        char    MADDR_VAL4a;
        char    MADDR_VAL5a;
        char    MADDR_VAL6a;
} StartupBuffer =
        {                                  /* Setup 2 receive buffers    */
```

```c
    NMA$C_PCLI_BFN, 2,               /* Register for user protocol   */
    NMA$C_PCLI_PTY, 0x0660,          /* 1500 byte receive buffer     */
    NMA$C_PCLI_BUS, 1500,            /* Frame padding disabled       */
    NMA$C_PCLI_PAD, NMA$C_STATE_OFF, /* Promiscuous disabled         */
    NMA$C_PCLI_PRM, NMA$C_STATE_OFF, /* Ethernet frame format        */
    NMA$C_PCLI_FMT, NMA$C_LINFM_ETH, /* Multicast mode off           */
    NMA$C_PCLI_MLT, NMA$C_STATE_OFF, /* Filter multicast address     */
    NMA$C_PCLI_MCA,
                    (short)sizeof(short)+6,   /* Size of counted string */
                    (short)NMA$C_LINMC_SET,   /* Set the address        */
                    0xab,0x00,0x00,0x04,0x00,0x01   /* Multicast address */
    };

struct
    {
    int size;
    int addr;
    } StartupBufferDescriptor =
    {
    sizeof(StartupBuffer),    /* Size and address of startup  */
    &StartupBuffer            /* buffer                       */
```

```c
};

struct dsc$descriptor_s devicedescriptor =        /* Device name descriptor        */
          { 0, DSC$K_DTYPE_T, DSC$K_CLASS_S, 0};

                                                  /* Assign the respective device  */
for (i=0, status = 0; (status != 1) && (device[i][0] != '*') ; i++)
{

    devicedescriptor.dsc$a_pointer = device[i];
    devicedescriptor.dsc$w_length = strlen(device[i]);
    status = sys$assign(&devicedescriptor, &channel, 0, 0);

}

if (!(status & 1)) lib$stop(status);
    printf("Controller %s\n",device[i-1]);

                                                  /* Start the controller          */
status = sys$qiow(0, channel, IO$_SETMODE + IO$M_STARTUP + IO$M_CTRL,
                  iosb, 0, 0, 0, &StartupBufferDescriptor, 0, 0, 0, 0);
printf("QIO Status : %d\n",status);

if (!(status & 1)) lib$stop(status);
if ((iosb[0] & 1) != 1)
{
    printf("STARTUP ERROR = %d %d %d %d\n",
           iosb[0], iosb[1], iosb[2], iosb[3]);
    printf("            = %2x %2x %2x\n",
```

```
                iosb[0], iosb[1], iosb[2], iosb[3]);

        exit(iosb[0]);

    }

/*--------------------------------------------------------------*/
/* checkwriteether()                                            */
/*--------------------------------------------------------------*/
/* This function simply reads a packet matching the mcast adrs and protocol */
/*--------------------------------------------------------------*/
int checkwriteether(char descr[27])
{
    int i;

    printf("RECEIVING\n");
    printf("Checking\n");

    status = sys$qiow(0, channel, IO$_READLBLK, iosb, 0, 0,      /*Read and WAIT for a matching packet  */
                      &buffer[14], sizeof(buffer)-14, 0, 0, &buffer[0], 0);

    printf("DATA : %s\n",&buffer[14]);
    memcpy(descr,&buffer[14],24);
    descr[24]='\0';

    if (!(status & 1))
    {
        lib$stop(status);
```

```c
        }
    if (iosb[0] != 1)
        {
            printf("ERROR = %2x %2x %2x %2x\n",
                        iosb[0], iosb[1], iosb[2], iosb[3]);
                lib$stop(iosb[0]);
        }
    return iosb[1] + 14;            /*Return the number of bytes transferred*/
}
/*-------------------------------------------------------------------*/
/* writeether()                                                      */
/*-------------------------------------------------------------------*/
/* This function writes a packet to the ethernet                     */
/*-------------------------------------------------------------------*/
int writeether(char xmitinfo[13])
{
    int i;

    char  xmtp5[8] = {0xab,0x00,0x04,0x01,0x02,0x60,0x06};    /* Server multicast addresses    */
    char  xmtbuf[14] = {0x00,0x00,0x00,0x00,0x00,0x00,0x00,0x00,
                        0x00,0x00,0x00,0x00,0x00,0x00};

    printf("SENDING\n");

    memcpy(xmtbuf,xmitinfo,13);
    status = sys$qiow(0, channel, IO$_WRITELBLK, iosb, 0, 0,    /* Write using a Wait    */
```

```c
                              &xmtbuf[0], sizeof(xmtbuf), 0, 0, &xmtp5[0], 0);

if (!(status & 1))
{
        lib$stop(status);
}

if (iosb[0] != 1)
{
        printf("ERROR = %2x %2x %2x %2x\n",
               iosb[0], iosb[1], iosb[2], iosb[3]);
        lib$stop(iosb[0]);
}
return iosb[1] + 14;            /* Return number of bytes transferred        */
}

/*-------------------------------------------------------------------------*/
/* main()
/*-------------------------------------------------------------------------*/
main()
{
char    descr[25];
int i;
char    recid[10][13] = {"REC1248VAL", "REC1249VAL", "REC1250VAL",
                         "REC1251VAL", "REC1252VAL", "REC1253VAL",
                         "REC1254VAL", "REC1255VAL", "REC1256VAL",
                         "REC1257VAL"};

controller();
```

```c
    for (i=0;i<10;i++)
    {
        writeether(&recid[i][0]);
        checkwriteether(descr);
        printf("DESCR : %s\n",descr);
    }
}
```

```c
/* SERVER.C */
#include <descrip.h>                          /* String descriptor types            */
#include <stdio.h>                            /* Standard Input Output header        */
#include <iodef.h>                            /* Input Output definitions            */
#include <string.h>
#include <stdlib.h>

#include "disk02:[edward.library]database.inc"  /* Database functions include file   */

/* Extracted from SYS$LIBRARY:LIB.REQ */
#define NMA$C_PCLI_PTY 2830                   /* Protocol identifier                 */
#define NMA$C_PCLI_PRM 2840                   /* Promiscuous mode identifier         */
#define NMA$C_PCLI_BFN 1105                   /* Receive buffer allocation identifier */
#define NMA$C_PCLI_BUS 2801                   /* Respective rcv buffer size          */
#define NMA$C_PCLI_PHA 2820                   /* Port address                        */
#define NMA$C_PCLI_PAD 2842                   /* Frame padding identifier            */
#define NMA$C_PCLI_FMT 2770                   /* Frame format                        */
```

```c
#define NMA$C_PCLI_MLT 2841          /* Multicast mode identifier         */
#define NMA$C_PCLI_MCA 2831          /* Multicast address definition      */

#define NMA$C_STATE_ON 0             /* State mode enabled                */
#define NMA$C_STATE_OFF 1            /* State mode disabled               */

#define NMA$C_LINMC_SET 1            /* Set multicast address             */
#define NMA$C_LINMC_CLR 2            /* Clear the multicast addresses     */
#define NMA$C_LINMC_CAL 3            /* Clear all multicast addresses     */

#define NMA$C_LINFM_ETH 1            /* Ethernet format                   */

int status;
short channel;
short iosb[4];
unsigned char buffer[1500];

/*-------------------------------------------------------------------*/
/* controller()                                                      */
/*-------------------------------------------------------------------*/
/* Open the ethernet controller.                                     */
/*-------------------------------------------------------------------*/
void controller()
{
    char device[5][6] = {"XEA0:", "XQA0:", "ESA0:", "ETA0:", "*"};
    int i, stat;

    struct
    {
```

```
short    BFN;
long     BFN_VAL;
short    PTY;
long     PTY_VAL;
short    BUS;
long     BUS_VAL;
short    PAD;
long     PAD_VAL;
short    PRM;
int      PRM_VAL;
short    ETH;
long     ETH_VAL;
short    MLT;
long     MLT_VAL;
short    MADDR;
short    MADDR_SIZEa;
short    MADDR_CMDa;
char     MADDR_VAL1a;
char     MADDR_VAL2a;
char     MADDR_VAL3a;
char     MADDR_VAL4a;
char     MADDR_VAL5a;
char     MADDR_VAL6a;
char     MADDR_VAL1b;
char     MADDR_VAL2b;
char     MADDR_VAL3b;
char     MADDR_VAL4b;
char     MADDR_VAL5b;
char     MADDR_VAL6b;

}StartupBuffer =
```

```
{
                NMA$C_PCLI_BFN,  2,                 /* Setup 2 receive buffers        */
                NMA$C_PCLI_PTY,  0x0660,            /* Register for user protocol     */
                NMA$C_PCLI_BUS,  1500,              /* 1500 byte receive buffer       */
                NMA$C_PCLI_PAD,  NMA$C_STATE_OFF,   /* Frame padding disabled         */
                NMA$C_PCLI_PRM,  NMA$C_STATE_OFF,   /* Promiscuous mode disabled      */
                NMA$C_PCLI_FMT,  NMA$C_LINFM_ETH,   /* Ethernet frame format          */
                NMA$C_PCLI_MLT,  NMA$C_STATE_OFF,   /* Multicast mode off             */
                NMA$C_PCLI_MCA,                     /* Filter multicast address       */
                (short)sizeof(short)+12,            /* Size of counted string         */
                (short)NMA$C_LINMC_SET,             /* Set the address                */
                                                    /* Multicast address1 for server  */
                0xab,0x00,0x04,0x01,0x01,
                                                    /* Multicast address2 for server */
                0xab,0x00,0x04,0x01,0x02
};

struct
{
    int size;
    int addr;
```

```c
} StartupBufferDescriptor =
    {
        sizeof(StartupBuffer),          /* Size and address of startup   */
        &StartupBuffer                  /* buffer                        */
    };

struct dsc$descriptor_s devicedescriptor =      /* Device name descriptor   */
                            { 0, DSC$K_DTYPE_T, DSC$K_CLASS_S, 0};

                                        /* Assign the respective device  */
for (i=0, status = 0; (status != 1) && (device[i][0] != '*') ; i++)
    {
    devicedescriptor.dsc$a_pointer = device[i];
    devicedescriptor.dsc$w_length = strlen(device[i]);
    status = sys$assign(&devicedescriptor, &channel, 0, 0);
    }

if (!(status & 1)) lib$stop(status);
    printf("Controller %s\n",device[i-1]);
                                        /* Start the controller          */
status = sys$qiow(0, channel, IO$_SETMODE + IO$M_STARTUP + IO$M_CTRL,
                  iosb, 0, 0, 0, &StartupBufferDescriptor, 0, 0, 0, 0);
printf("QIO Status : %d\n",status);

if (!(status & 1)) lib$stop(status);
if ((iosb[0] & 1) != 1)
    {
```

```c
            printf("STARTUP ERROR = %d %d %d %d\n",
                        iosb[0], iosb[1], iosb[2], iosb[3]);
            printf("        = %2x %2x %2x\n",
                        iosb[0], iosb[1], iosb[2], iosb[3]);

            exit(iosb[0]);

    }

/*-----------------------------------------------------------------------*/
/* checkwriteether()
/*-----------------------------------------------------------------------*/
/* This function simply reads the ethernet controller
/*-----------------------------------------------------------------------*/
int checkwriteether(char recid[13])
{
    int i;

    printf("RECEIVING\n");
    printf("Checking\n");
    stat = sys$qiow(0, chan, IO$_READLBLK, iosb, 0, 0,
                    &buffer[14], sizeof(buffer)-14, 0, 0, &buffer[0], 0);

    printf("DATA : %s\n",&buffer[14]);
    memcpy(recid,&buffer[14],13); recid[12]='\0';

    if (!(stat & 1))
    {
        lib$stop(stat);
    }

    if (iosb[0] != 1)
```

```c
        {
            printf("ERROR = %2x %2x %2x\n",
                   iosb[0], iosb[1], iosb[2], iosb[3]);

            lib$stop(iosb[0]);
        }
        return iosb[1] + 14;
}

/*-------------------------------------------------------------------*/
/* writeether()                                                      */
/*-------------------------------------------------------------------*/
/* This function writes a packet to the ethernet                     */
/*-------------------------------------------------------------------*/
int writeether(char xmitinfo[27])
{
        int i;

        char xmtp5[8] = {0xab,0x00,0x00,0x04,0x00,0x01,0x60,0x06};  /* Client multicast address */
        char xmtbuf[28] = {0x00,0x00,0x00,0x00,0x00,0x00,0x00,0x00,0x00,0x00,
                           0x00,0x00,0x00,0x00,0x00,0x00,0x00,0x00,0x00,0x00,
                           0x00,0x00,0x00,0x00,0x00,0x00,0x00,0x00};

        printf("SENDING\n");

        memcpy(xmtbuf,xmitinfo,24);

        stat = sys$qiow(0, chan, IO$_WRITELBLK, iosb, 0, 0,
                        &xmtbuf[0], sizeof(xmtbuf), 0, 0, &xmtp5[0], 0);

        if (!(stat & 1))
```

```c
        {
        lib$stop(stat);
        }

    if (iosb[0] != 1)
        {
        printf("ERROR = %2x %2x %2x %2x\n",
                iosb[0], iosb[1], iosb[2], iosb[3]);
        lib$stop(iosb[0]);
        }

    return iosb[1] + 14;

    }
/*-------------------------------------------------------------------------------------
/* main()
/*-------------------------------------------------------------------------------------*/
main()
    {
    char  recid[13];
    char  descr[25];
    struct info info_struct;

    controller();
    for (;;)
        {
        checkwriteether(recid);
        get_select_rec(recid,info_struct);
        strncpy(descr,info_struct.descr,24);
        writeether(descr);

        }
    }
```

7

Broadcasting

Broadcasting is akin to multicasting in that it operates utilizing a connectionless communication method. As before, there exist no logical links between processes but instead there are broadcasts to all nodes on the network. Simply put, instead of directing a packet to one node or a group of nodes, every registered node on the local network receives the frame for use in the local machine. As an example, let's look at a simple application in a system that contains several nodes that maintain receiver processes. A transmitter process on a node would submit a frame that has a destination address of FF-FF-FF-FF-FF-FF. Every node with a BCAST receiver process would accept the frame and process it accordingly.

What should be noticed under BCAST is that it is very similar to MCAST in the way that certain functions are performed. The one similarity between BCAST and MCAST is that a broadcast address is registered as a multicast address in the same manner that multicast addresses are registered for a process. Note also the protocol registration; it is handled the same way that protocols are registered under MCAST. The primary difference is that of the destination address given to a frame and how the frames are processed and distributed in the network. As was stated earlier in this book, every communications method, so far as the base functions are concerned, is very similar. This adds the ability to convert easily between communication methods as well as combine multiple communication methods.

Figure 7.1 depicts the general structure of BCAST in a general-purpose environment. As can be seen, every process contains a destination address of FF-FF-FF-FF-FF-FF and a protocol of 0x0660. Assume that ProcessA submits a frame for the destination FF-FF-FF-FF-FF-FF with protocol 0x0660; every process on the network registered with the broadcast address and protocol would intercept that frame. As stated, in some ways this type of connectionless communication emulates MCAST except that under BCAST the transmitting process communicates with every registered receive process on the network.

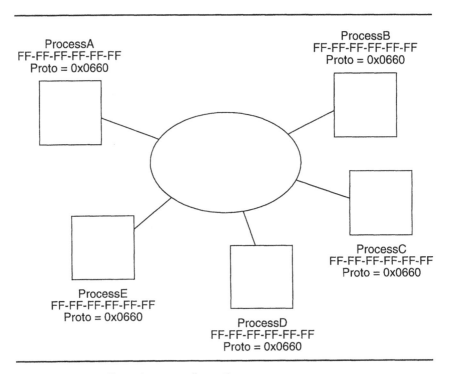

Figure 7.1. Broadcast configuration.

PHASES OF BCAST

If an understanding of MCAST has been established, then BCAST will be very easy to grasp. Remember, the only difference with respect to communications between MCAST and BCAST is that instead of communicating with a few nodes, a process can now communicate with every registered node. This section will outline the phases involved in BCAST in a simple and straightforward manner. In order to assist in the explanation, periodic comparisons will be made to MCAST in order to show the similarities as well as differences. Since BCAST is so much simpler than MCAST, the phases to be explained will simply follow that of MCAST, which, as before, may be varied to suit the specific needs of the application at hand.

One important fact to remember is that a process on, for instance, NODE01 cannot use BCAST to talk to another process on the same node. Recall that under TIPC this was possible because a logical link was simply routed back around to the respective process on that node through the DNA of that node. Under BCAST, the transmitting process connects below the primary layers of DNA responsible for establishing the respective logical links to another process. What this means is that, as frames are being transmitted, that transmitting node cannot receive frames at the same time over the same physical device. This leads to the point that a frame sent to another process on the same node must use a higher level of communications such as TIPC.

BCAST Initiation

Before BCAST can be accomplished, the process must connect to the node's Ethernet device. This connection establishes a channel that is used for information transfer between the process and the device. As with MCAST, the format for the task specification string is simply the name of the device on the local node. See Table 7.1.

Once the channel to a controller has been returned from the System Service call, the controller's mode must then be set based on the desired operation to be performed. During this setup, a series of parameters are passed to the controller in order to de-

Table 7.1.   Device/controller names.

XEA0:	DEUNA and DELUA
XQA0:	DEQNA and DELQA
ETA0:	DEBNA
ESA0:	DESVA

fine the protocol, size of the I/O buffers, multicast mode state, promiscuous mode state, and broadcast address as well as a plethora of other functions that can be performed with the controller. For additional information as to the available functions that can be defined for the controller, refer to the *VMS I/O User's Reference Manual: Part II* and SYS$LIBRARY:LIB.REQ.

BCAST Transmission

In TIPC it was stated that transmission of data from one process to another occurs over a logical link between the processes. Under BCAST, as with MCAST, the channel is only available between a process and the controller. Once the information is passed out of the process along the channel for transmission, the controller performs standard transmission procedures and submits the packet to the network as a frame. In such a situation, a transmit process and receive processes do not have to cooperate to have information transferred across the network. A majority of the work is accomplished by the device connected to the channel of the process.

BCAST Reception

Once a node receives the frame, the physical layer passes the frame up to the data link layer. The DNA layers then perform the standard address comparisons to see if that frame is destined for the node. If a module exists within that node that accepts the protocol and the destination address of the packet, the information is passed up to that module, or process, for processing. If no module exists, the frame is not used.

BCAST Termination

In order to terminate a BCAST process, the process may issue a shutdown message to the controller over the channel. Once the call returns, the process should then simply deassign the channel. Recall that in TIPC the primary process and the process located at the other end of the channel should cooperate in the termination; however, since the channel is connected to a device, the device handles its own deassignment with the process on the channel.

IMPLEMENTATION

The following BCAST implementation takes into account the information previously discussed and incorporates actual code to assist in the explanation. The code, as will be seen, is similar to that of MCAST and was the basis for a general-purpose health check implementation for a client/server application. The idea behind this application was simply to send out a broadcast message and have it received by a registered receiving process. In the finished product, a primary process submitted a broadcast to find out who is available for information exchange. For this explanation, BCAST Transmitter and BCAST Receiver are reserved names for processes that transmit and receive broadcast messages and, as stated, are for this explanation only. The purpose of this naming convention is to identify the processes where, in actual implementations, BCAST is internal to the application. Later in this chapter, different paradigms will be made available for representation of other possible implementations of BCAST.

BCAST Transmitter

The BCAST Transmitter is responsible for submitting the broadcast message to the network. As was seen in the MCAST implementation, the BCAST Transmitter simply establishes a channel to a controller and sets the characteristics of that controller. For all practical purposes, the defines for the application are identical to the defines for MCAST, as seen in Figure 6.2 in the previous chapter.

Figure 7.2 contains the extended characteristics buffer, which is utilized in the controller() function of the transmitter. This structure is passed to the controller on startup to notify the device of its required operating characteristics for the channel attached to the process. Note that the characteristics are not shared with other processes/channels and only affect that one channel's characteristics for the process. As can be seen, the buffer is to notify the device that it should preallocate 2 (_BFN) 1500-byte (_BUS) receive buffers where the default is normally 1. This parameter is used to notify the device that it should maintain at least two frames when the process connected to the channel has no read requests queued to the device. Notice also that the padding (_PAD) of the Ethernet packet (_FMT) is disabled, which, as previously stated, allows for data to range from 46 to 1500 bytes with padding performed within the data portion of the frame. The remainder of the buffer maintains information used to register the process with a broadcast address, specific protocol, promiscuous mode state, and so forth.

As can be seen, the process is registered to receive protocol 0x0660 (_PTY) with the standard broadcast address of FF-FF-FF-FF-FF-FF (_MCA). The broadcast address parameter maintains a counted string buffer where the first parameter maintains the count of bytes available in the string and the second parameter may be _SET to set one or more multicast addresses, _CLR to clear specified addresses, or _CAL to clear all multicast addresses. In this instance, there is only one broadcast address; however, multicast addresses and the broadcast address may be intermingled on one machine allowing for communication characteristics for both MCAST and BCAST. The remaining elements of the parameter are the 6-byte multicast/broadcast addresses to set or clear, depending on the previous state parameter.

A final note to make here is that of the state of the promiscuous mode (_PRM) and multicast mode (_MLT) parameters. The state of these parameters depends on the implementation. For this implementation, multicast and promiscuous modes disabled, the process will receive only those packets with a protocol of 0x0660 and the stated destination broadcast address of FF-FF-FF-FF-FF-FF. If multicast is enabled, all multicast addresses will be accepted. If promiscuous mode is enabled, any and all packets will be

```
StartupBuffer =
{
                        /* Setup 2 receive buffers      */
    NMA$C_PCLI_BFN, 2,
                        /* Register for user protocol    */
    NMA$C_PCLI_PTY, 0x0660,
                        /* 1500 byte receive buffer      */
    NMA$C_PCLI_BUS, 1500,
                        /* Frame padding disabled       */
    NMA$C_PCLI_PAD, NMA$C_STATE_OFF,
                        /* Promiscuous disabled         */
    NMA$C_PCLI_PRM, NMA$C_STATE_OFF,
                        /* Ethernet frame format         */
    NMA$C_PCLI_FMT, NMA$C_LINFM_ETH,
                        /* Multicast mode off            */
    NMA$C_PCLI_MLT, NMA$C_STATE_OFF,
                        /* Filter multicast address      */
    NMA$C_PCLI_MCA,
                        /* Size of counted string        */
        (short)sizeof(short)+6,
                        /* Set the address               */
        (short)NMA$C_LINMC_SET,
                        /* Broadcast address             */
        0xff,0xff,0xff,0xff,0xff,0xff
};
```

Figure 7.2.   Extended characteristics buffer for startup.

accepted without regard to the protocol and multicast address registered for the process.

Notice in Figure 7.3 that an operation exists where it loops through a series of calls to SYS$ASSIGN in an attempt to attach to the device defined in the descriptor and create a channel. Once the channel is created, it is used in a call to SYS$QIOW in order to set up and start the controller for the channel. During the call to SYS$QIOW, the extended characteristics buffer is passed in P2 with functions for IO$_SETMODE and IO$M_STARTUP, which tells the device to start up with the modes specified in P2.

Once the controller is set up, the rest of the functions operate in a manner similar to that of MCAST and every other implementation to be introduced. As can be seen in Figure 7.4, two buffers are created for the transmission where one contains the

```
struct dsc$descriptor_s devicedescriptor =     /* Device name descriptor     */
            { 0, DSC$K_DTYPE_T, DSC$K_CLASS_S, 0};

                                                 /* Assign the respective device     */
for (i=0, status = 0; (status != 1) && (device[i][0] != '*') ; i++)
{
    devicedescriptor.dsc$a_pointer = device[i];
    devicedescriptor.dsc$w_length = strlen(device[i]);
    status = sys$assign(&devicedescriptor, &channel, 0, 0);
}

if (!(status & 1)) lib$stop(status);
    printf("Controller %s\n",device[i-1]);

                                                 /* Start the controller     */
status = sys$qiow(0, channel, IO$_SETMODE + IO$M_STARTUP + IO$M_CTRL,
                 iosb, 0, 0, 0, &StartupBufferDescriptor, 0, 0, 0, 0);
```

Figure 7.3. Controller startup.

```
char    xmtp5[8] = {0xff,0xff,0xff,0xff,0xff,0xff,0x60,0x06};
char    xmtbuf[14]= {0x00,0x00,0x00,0x00,0x00,0x00,0x00,0x00,
                     0x00,0x00,0x00,0x00,0x00,0x00};

printf("SENDING\n");

                        /* Write using a Wait            */
status = sys$qiow(0, channel, IO$_WRITELBLK, iosb, 0, 0,
           &xmtbuf[0], sizeof(xmtbuf), 0, 0, &xmtp5[0], 0);
```

Figure 7.4.   Transmission.

required destination address and protocol and the other contains
the data to transfer. In the figure, XMTP5 contains the destination broadcast address in the first 6 bytes while the last 2 bytes
contain the protocol. As can be seen, the protocol value is reversed from the previous declarations (i.e., 0x0660 → 6006) in
the extended characteristics buffer. This information is utilized
in assigning the information to the outgoing frame's fields for
proper routing of the information through the network.

The XMTBUF buffer allows the storage of up to 14 bytes for
transmission to all receive processes. This buffer was set up for
demonstration only and may be extended to the largest data field
size of the frame depending on the state of the padding (_PAD)
parameter. Now that the buffers are prepared and the data is
ready for transmission, the SYS$QIOW function is called to trans-
fer the information from the process, down the channel to the device. In the call to SYS$QIOW, the buffers are passed to the
function as well as the channel to the device and the function
IO$_WRITELBLK. The device then prepares the information into
a legitimate frame and submits it to the physical layer for transmission on the network.

BCAST Receiver

A BCAST receiver is the process that receives the broadcast messages from the BCAST transmitter. The definitions for the receiver for this implementation are identical to the definitions

```
status = sys$qiow(0, channel, IO$_READLBLK, iosb, 0, 0,
        &buffer[14], sizeof(buffer)-14, 0, 0, &buffer[0], 0);
```

Figure 7.5.   Reception.

depicted in Figure 6.2 in the previous chapter under MCAST.
The other identical characteristic of the receiver to the transmitter is that of the controller() function utilized to start up the
controller on the channel. All calls to the SYS$QIO System Ser-
vice function maintain the same buffers and operation as are
utilized in the transmitter except for the function specifier.

In order to receive information from the device, the SYS$QIOW
function is called with the IO$_READLBLK function. The re-
ceived information is then placed into a set of buffers for utilization of the information within the process. As can be seen in Figure
7.5, The P1 buffer of the SYS$QIOW call receives the data field of
the frame. P2 maintains the size of the information required to be
retrieved and placed into the buffer of P1. P5 maintains a buffer to
capture the header of the frame, specifically the source and destination address as well as the protocol of the frame.

BCAST Output

Now that the source code has been reviewed for the BCAST receiver and transmitter, let's review the output of the BCAST receiver and see what happens during each step. As can be seen in
Table 7.2, the first step is to connect a channel to the controller to
start up and set the mode of the controller, as can be noted with the
Controller: ESA0: output. The next step is to issue a receive request to the controller in order to attempt to receive a frame denoted by RECEIVING followed by Checking and then a frame's
header output. The destination address (D) contains the broadcast
address, while the source address (S) of the frame is the address of
the transmitting node. The protocol value of 0x0660 is the value
assigned to the frame for transmission to the receiver, which is
registered to receive the said protocol.

Table 7.2.   Sample output.

```
Controller : ESA0:
QIO Status : 1
RECEIVING
Checking
D: ff ff ff ff ff ff / S: aa 00 04 00 58 06 / P: 60-06
RECEIVING
Checking
D: ff ff ff ff ff ff / S: aa 00 04 00 58 06 / P: 60-06
```

PARADIGMS

In order to present workable situations for BCAST, this communication method will be, in some instances, incorporated with previous examples outlined under MCAST. TIPC allows the DNA to handle any peripheral message-passing, so incorporating BCAST is really not useful in that situation. Since BCAST and MCAST are of the same family, the following explanation will be much easier to understand than in previous sections. In order to follow the methods outlined, the MCAST client/server and a peer-to-peer method will be reviewed with BCAST extensions to add features to the implementation. There are additonal implementations for BCAST; however, in these examples the BCAST explanation will be limited to provide a better understanding of the technique as a whole.

Peer-to-Peer

A peer-to-peer implementation is much easier to implement with BCAST than it is under MCAST. As before, independent systems on separate nodes occasionally perform health checks with each other to determine the states of the respective nodes/systems. Using BCAST simply replaces the MCAST implementation outlined in the previous section; however, because of the basic definition of BCAST, this type of application is more suitable for BCAST's characteristics.

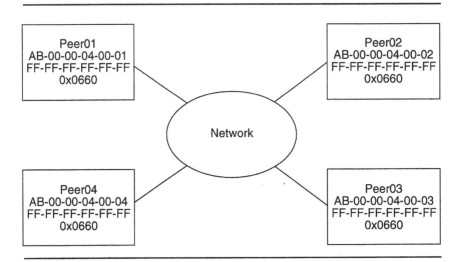

Figure 7.6.   Peer-to-peer configuration.

As can be seen in Figure 7.6, four independent systems exist that perform the same function but operate as redundant back-ups to each other. In order to maintain a backup scheme such as this, all nodes must receive and process the information; however, only one node can respond based on the result of the processing. In this instance, all four nodes maintain the broadcast address while also maintaining unique multicast addresses. When information is destined for an information processor, it will accept the information (based on the protocol and address). Once the information has been processed, a result based on the specific information must be sent out onto the network. If all four nodes responded simultaneously, there would obviously be wasted network utilization, not to mention the confusion at the destination node of the outgoing frame. What should be noticed here is that the example is a combination of MCAST and BCAST in order to demonstrate the ability of communicating between peer processes as BCAST and MCAST to specific processes. This adds some interesting possibilities in that one process can communicate with one or all processes without knowing the precise nodal address of the destination processes.

Periodically, health checks are performed between the processes. In order to perform this health check, each node must perform the check to determine which nodes are active information processors. Let's assume that Peer01 is initially the primary processor. On occasion, each node will send out a hello request message in a frame destined for the broadcast address. Once this frame is received by the other three nodes, these nodes respond to the Peer01 MCAST address with an acknowledgment frame. Once Peer01 receives the frames, the source addresses are registered in a database in order to maintain the means of knowing the states of all peers during each hello poll. If at any time a node should either respond with a negative status or not respond to a hello poll, that node will be assumed to be inactive. At that instant, if the inactive node was the primary processor, the next node in the hierarchy of redundant backups will assume the responsibility of the primary processor. In this instance, Peer02 would become primary processor.

Client/Server

In this explanation of a client/server (monitor) implementation, the MCAST client/server implementation will be supplemented by the BCAST communications implementation. The reason for this explanation is due to the fact that BCAST alone is not the best communications scheme for the client/server paradigm. Recall that such a paradigm involves a centralized data server that is interrogated by a series of client processes for information management purposes.

The most useful paradigm for BCAST is with the MCAST client-aware implementation. Recall that a client-aware implementation takes into account the fact that the server is aware of all currently available clients. This type of implementation is created by having a series of clients that send a hello message to the server(s) when they are initialized, and is useful in a distributed processing environment where processing is truly distributed on several different nodes. If MCAST is used exclusively, the client process must know either the explicit or multicast address of the server beforehand to send a message to register itself with that server. By incorporating BCAST, the client simply sub-

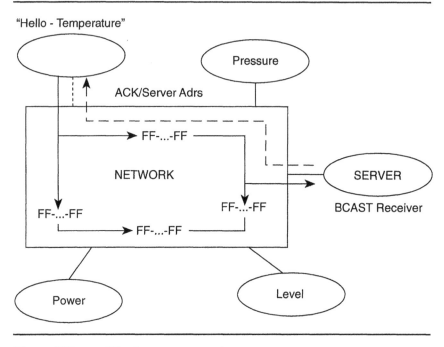

Figure 7.7.   Client-aware scenario.

mits a broadcast message to the network where the server is registered as a BCAST receiver. Once the server receives the broadcast frame, it registers the source address of the frame and sends a response back to that client to notify the client of the server's address.

As can be seen in Figure 7.7, the server would act as a traffic cop in order to send the correct information to the client that is to process the information. When a client becomes active or is initialized, it would send a broadcast message stating that it is responsible for temperature measurement processing and management. The server would register the client's address and related information in a local database for routing purposes and return an acknowledgment to the client as part of a message containing the server's address. From this point on, any information transfer between any client and the server can be direct, since, during the broadcast, the server became aware of the client's address and, during the server's acknowledgment, the client became aware of the server's address.

Another interesting application for BCAST involves the propagation of information to all related client processes when the server receives an update of information. This type of BCAST application is very simple to implement and takes care of users in such a multiuser environment. As can be seen in Figure 7.8, a

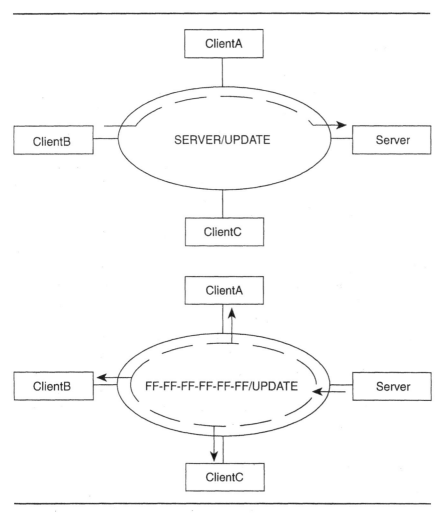

Figure 7.8. Message propagation.

client sends an update to the server in order to update the contents of, for example, a record in a database maintained by the server. Once the record is updated, the server sends a broadcast out to all client processes notifying the processes of the new contents of the record. This type of update propagation takes into account the fact that one of the clients may be viewing that particular record and will require updates as they become available. In such an instance, the client viewing that record will accept that broadcast information and update the user interface for the user.

DEVELOPMENT

One idea to maintain while developing a BCAST-oriented application is that broadcasting is not an automatic type of communication implementation. As mentioned in the *VMS I/O User's Reference Manual: Part II*, in order to have a broadcast receiver, the process must have the broadcast address registered in the same manner as multicast address registration. One other point to keep in mind is that a broadcast-oriented implementation is not best to implement as the only available communications situation. BCAST tends to be best suited for communicating with every related process, as in health check and peer-to-peer implementations. In a case where BCAST is the primary communication method, there tends to be additional overhead in handling the information associated with the broadcast frame, since every related process must process that respective frame and no directional message management is possible. As was seen in the client/server example, BCAST is suited for client startup situations in order to provide the means of establishing the addresses of the applications. In a peer-to-peer implementation, BCAST lends itself to the fact that all related peers can communicate with each other with one frame instead of communicating with each peer using one frame per related peer.

SAMPLE BCAST APPLICATION

The following pages contain source code for two applications that can be utilized to test a small BCAST implementation. The first set of code contains the source for the BCAST transmitter, while the second set of code maintains the BCAST receiver. The idea behind this implementation is to have one process periodically send a broadcast message to the network while the receiver simply reads the messages and displays header information from the message's frame. For best results, you should run two or more BCAST transmitters and one or more BCAST receivers in order to see the full effect of the ideas of BCAST.

```c
/* BROADCAST_OUT.C */
#include <descrip.h>          /* String descriptor types             */
#include <stdio.h>            /* Standard Input Output header        */
#include <iodef.h>            /* Input Output definitions            */
#include <string.h>
#include <stdlib.h>

/* Extracted from SYS$LIBRARY:LIB.REQ */
#define NMA$C_PCLI_PTY 2830   /* Protocol identifier                 */
#define NMA$C_PCLI_PRM 2840   /* Promiscuous mode identifier         */
#define NMA$C_PCLI_BFN 1105   /* Receive buffer allocation identifier */
#define NMA$C_PCLI_BUS 2801   /* Respective rcv buffer size          */
#define NMA$C_PCLI_PHA 2820   /* Port address                        */
#define NMA$C_PCLI_PAD 2842   /* Frame padding identifier            */
#define NMA$C_PCLI_FMT 2770   /* Frame format                        */
#define NMA$C_PCLI_MLT 2841   /* Multicast mode identifier           */
#define NMA$C_PCLI_MCA 2831   /* Multicast address definition        */

#define NMA$C_STATE_ON 0      /* State mode enabled                  */
#define NMA$C_STATE_OFF 1     /* State mode disabled                 */

#define NMA$C_LINMC_SET 1     /* Set multicast address               */
#define NMA$C_LINMC_CLR 2     /* Clear the multicast addresses       */
#define NMA$C_LINMC_CAL 3     /* Clear all multicast addresses       */

#define NMA$C_LINFM_ETH 1     /* Ethernet format                     */

int status;
```

```c
unsigned char buffer[1500];

/*-------------------------------------------------------------------------*/
/* controller()                                                            */
/*-------------------------------------------------------------------------*/
/* Open the ethernet controller.                                           */
/*-------------------------------------------------------------------------*/
void controller()
{
    char device[5][6] = {"XEA0:", "XQA0:", "ESA0:", "ETA0:", "*"};
    int i, status;
    struct
    {
        short       BFN;
        long        BFN_VAL;
        short       PTY;
        long        PTY_VAL;
        short       BUS;
        long        BUS_VAL;
        short       PAD;
        long        PAD_VAL;
        short       PRM;
        int         PRM_VAL;
        short       ETH;
        long        ETH_VAL;
        short       MLT;
        long        MLT_VAL;
        short       MADDR;
        short       MADDR_SIZEa;
        short       MADDR_CMDa;
        char        MADDR_VAL1a;
```

```
        char    MADDR_VAL2a;
        char    MADDR_VAL3a;
        char    MADDR_VAL4a;
        char    MADDR_VAL5a;
        char    MADDR_VAL6a;
} StartupBuffer =
        {

        NMA$C_PCLI_BFN, 2,              /* Setup 2 receive buffers        */

        NMA$C_PCLI_PTY, 0x0660,         /* Register for user protocol     */

        NMA$C_PCLI_BUS, 1500,           /* 1500 byte receive buffer       */

        NMA$C_PCLI_PAD, NMA$C_STATE_OFF,  /* Frame padding disabled       */

        NMA$C_PCLI_PRM, NMA$C_STATE_OFF,  /* Promiscuous disabled         */

        NMA$C_PCLI_FMT, NMA$C_LINFM_ETH,  /* Ethernet frame format        */

        NMA$C_PCLI_MLT, NMA$C_STATE_OFF,  /* Multicast mode off           */

        NMA$C_PCLI_MCA,                 /* Filter multicast address       */

                                        /* Size of counted string         */
        (short)sizeof(short)+6,
                                        /* Set the address                */
        (short)NMA$C_LINMC_SET,
                                        /* Broadcast address              */
        0xff,0xff,0xff,0xff,0xff,0xff

        };
```

```
struct
{
     int size;
     int addr;
} StartupBufferDescriptor =
     {
        sizeof(StartupBuffer),         /* Size and address of startup   */
        &StartupBuffer                 /* buffer                        */
     };

struct dsc$descriptor_s devicedescriptor =        /* Device name descriptor */
                          { 0, DSC$K_DTYPE_T, DSC$K_CLASS_S, 0};

for (i=0, status = 0; (status != 1) && (device[i][0] != '*') ; i++)   /* Assign the respective device */
{
     devicedescriptor.dsc$a_pointer = device[i];
     devicedescriptor.dsc$w_length = strlen(device[i]);
     status = sys$assign(&devicedescriptor, &channel, 0, 0);
}

if (!(status & 1)) lib$stop(status);
     printf("Controller %s\n",device[i-1]);

                          /* Start the controller */
status = sys$qiow(0, channel, IO$_SETMODE + IO$M_STARTUP + IO$M_CTRL,
                  iosb, 0, 0, 0, &StartupBufferDescriptor, 0, 0, 0, 0);
```

```c
        printf("QIO Status : %d\n",status);

        if (!(status & 1)) lib$stop(status);
        if ((iosb[0] & 1) != 1)
        {
            printf("STARTUP ERROR = %d %d %d\n",
                    iosb[0], iosb[1], iosb[2], iosb[3]);
            printf(" = %2x %2x %2x\n",
                    iosb[0], iosb[1], iosb[2], iosb[3]);
            exit(iosb[0]);
        }
}
/*----------------------------------------------------------*/
/* writeether()                                             */
/*----------------------------------------------------------*/
/* This function writes a packet to the ethernet            */
/*----------------------------------------------------------*/
int writeether()
{
    int i;

    char  xmtp5[8] = {0xff,0xff,0xff,0xff,0xff,0x60,0x06};            /* Broadcast address      */
    char  xmtbuf[14] = {0x00,0x00,0x00,0x00,0x00,0x00,0x00,
                        0x00,0x00,0x00,0x00,0x00,0x00,0x00};

    printf("SENDING\n");

    status = sys$qiow(0, channel, IO$_WRITELBLK, iosb, 0, 0,          /* Write using a Wait     */
```

```c
                     &xmtbuf[0], sizeof(xmtbuf), 0, 0, &xmtp5[0], 0);

    if (!(status & 1))
    {
        lib$stop(status);
    }

    if (iosb[0] != 1)
    {
        printf("ERROR = %2x %2x %2x %2x\n",
               iosb[0], iosb[1], iosb[2], iosb[3]);
        lib$stop(iosb[0]);
    }

    return iosb[1] + 14;        /* Return number of bytes transferred    */
}

/*---------------------------------------------------------------*/
/* main()                                                        */
/*---------------------------------------------------------------*/
main()
{
    int i;

    controller();
    for (i=0;i<100;i++)
    {
        writeether();
        sleep(5);
    }
}
```

177

```c
/* BROADCAST_IN.C */
#include <descrip.h>                            /* String descriptor types       */
#include <stdio.h>                              /* Standard Input Output header   */
#include <iodef.h>                              /* Input Output definitions       */
#include <string.h>
#include <stdlib.h>

    /* Database functions include file    */
#include "disk02:[edward.library]database.inc"

/* Extracted from SYS$LIBRARY:LIB.REQ */
#define NMA$C_PCLI_PTY 2830                     /* Protocol identifier                      */
#define NMA$C_PCLI_PRM 2840                     /* Promiscuous mode identifier              */
#define NMA$C_PCLI_BFN 1105                     /* Receive buffer allocation identifier     */
#define NMA$C_PCLI_BUS 2801                     /* Respective rcv buffer size               */
#define NMA$C_PCLI_PHA 2820                     /* Port address                             */
#define NMA$C_PCLI_PAD 2842                     /* Frame padding identifier                 */
#define NMA$C_PCLI_FMT 2770                     /* Frame format                             */
#define NMA$C_PCLI_MLT 2841                     /* Multicast mode identifier                */
#define NMA$C_PCLI_MCA 2831                     /* Multicast address definition             */

#define NMA$C_STATE_ON 0                        /* State mode enabled                       */
#define NMA$C_STATE_OFF 1                       /* State mode disabled                      */

#define NMA$C_LINMC_SET 1                       /* Set multicast address                    */
#define NMA$C_LINMC_CLR 2                       /* Clear the multicast addresses            */
#define NMA$C_LINMC_CAL 3                       /* Clear all multicast addresses            */

#define NMA$C_LINFM_ETH 1                       /* Ethernet format                          */
```

```c
int status;
short channel;
short iosb[4];
unsigned char buffer[1500];

/*--------------------------------------------------------*/
/* controller()                                           */
/*--------------------------------------------------------*/
/* Open the ethernet controller.                          */
/*--------------------------------------------------------*/

void controller()
{
    char device[5][6] = {"XEA0:", "XQA0:", "ESA0:", "ETA0:", "*"};
    int i, stat;

    struct
    {
        short   BFN;
        long    BFN_VAL;
        short   PTY;
        long    PTY_VAL;
        short   BUS;
        long    BUS_VAL;
        short   PAD;
        long    PAD_VAL;
        short   PRM;
        int     PRM_VAL;
        short   ETH;
        long    ETH_VAL;
        short   MLT;
        long    MLT_VAL;
```

```c
    short  MADDR;
    short  MADDR_SIZEa;
    short  MADDR_CMDa;
    char   MADDR_VAL1a;
    char   MADDR_VAL2a;
    char   MADDR_VAL3a;
    char   MADDR_VAL4a;
    char   MADDR_VAL5a;
    char   MADDR_VAL6a;
} StartupBuffer =
    {

    NMA$C_PCLI_BFN,  2,                 /* Setup 2 receive buffers       */
    NMA$C_PCLI_PTY,  0x0660,            /* Register for user protocol    */
    NMA$C_PCLI_BUS,  1500,              /* 1500 byte receive buffer      */
    NMA$C_PCLI_PAD,  NMA$C_STATE_OFF,   /* Frame padding disabled        */
    NMA$C_PCLI_PRM,  NMA$C_STATE_OFF,   /* Promiscuous mode disabled     */
    NMA$C_PCLI_FMT,  NMA$C_LINFM_ETH,   /* Ethernet frame format         */
    NMA$C_PCLI_MLT,  NMA$C_STATE_OFF,   /* Multicast mode off            */
    NMA$C_PCLI_MCA,                     /* Filter multicast address      */
        (short)sizeof(short)+6,         /* Size of counted string        */
        (short)NMA$C_LINMC_SET,         /* Set the address               */
```

```c
struct
{
        int size;
        int addr;                              /* Broadcast address    */
                                               0xff,0xff,0xff,0xff,0xff,0xff
} StartupBufferDescriptor =
{
        sizeof(StartupBuffer),                 /* Size and address of startup */
        &StartupBuffer                         /* buffer                      */
};

struct dsc$descriptor_s devicedescriptor =     /* Device name descriptor  */
        { 0, DSC$K_DTYPE_T, DSC$K_CLASS_S, 0};

                                               /* Assign the respective device  */
for (i=0, status = 0; (status != 1) && (device[i][0] != '*') ; i++)
{
        devicedescriptor.dsc$a_pointer = device[i];
        devicedescriptor.dsc$w_length = strlen(device[i]);
        status = sys$assign(&devicedescriptor, &channel, 0, 0);
}

if (!(status & 1)) lib$stop(status);
        printf("Controller %s\n",device[i-1]);

                                               /* Start the controller  */
```

```c
    status = sys$qiow(0, channel, IO$_SETMODE + IO$M_STARTUP + IO$M_CTRL,
                      iosb, 0, 0, 0, &StartupBufferDescriptor, 0, 0, 0, 0);
    printf("QIO Status : %d\n",status);

    if (!(status & 1)) lib$stop(status);
    if ((iosb[0] & 1) != 1)
    {
        printf("STARTUP ERROR = %d %d %d %d\n",
               iosb[0], iosb[1], iosb[2], iosb[3]);
        printf(" = %2x %2x %2x\n",
               iosb[0], iosb[1], iosb[2], iosb[3]);
        exit(iosb[0]);
    }
}
/*-----------------------------------------------------------------*/
/* checkwriteether()                                               */
/*-----------------------------------------------------------------*/
/* This function simply reads the ethernet controller              */
/*-----------------------------------------------------------------*/
int checkwriteether()
{
    int i;

    printf("RECEIVING\n");
    printf("Checking\n");
    stat = sys$qiow(0, chan, IO$_READLBLK, iosb, 0, 0,
                    &buffer[14], sizeof(buffer)-14, 0, 0, &buffer[0], 0);

                    /* Output the buffer */
    printf("D: %2x %2x %2x %2x %2x / S: %2x %2x %2x %2x %2x %2x / P: %2x-%2x\n",
           buffer[0],buffer[1],buffer[2],buffer[3],buffer[4],buffer[5]);
```

```c
            buffer[6],buffer[7],buffer[8],buffer[9],buffer[10],buffer[11],
            buffer[12],buffer[13]);

    if (!(stat & 1))
    {
        lib$stop(stat);
    }

    if (iosb[0] != 1)
    {
        printf("ERROR = %2x %2x %2x %2x\n",
                iosb[0], iosb[1], iosb[2], iosb[3]);
        lib$stop(iosb[0]);
    }

    return iosb[1] + 14;
}

/*--------------------------------------------------------------------
/* main()
/*------------------------------------------------------------------*/
main()
{
    int i;

    controller();
    for (i=0;i<100;i++)
    {
        checkwriteether();
    }
}
```

8

Explicit Addressing

Explicit addressing performs connectionless-oriented communications directly between two nodes. This method is a combination of the ideas behind TIPC and the connectionless methods of MCAST/BCAST. The primary purpose of EADRS is to exploit the flexible nature of connectionless communications while utilizing the directional messaging capabilities similar to TIPC. Directional messaging does not mean that the packet goes directly to the node; it means only that one node with the destination address of the frame will process the frame. The one point to notice during this discussion is that the destination is a legitimate Ethernet address (AA-00-04-00-xx-xx) and not a multicast address. As with other communication methods presented in this book, the functions of the respective EADRS processes are the same as that of MCAST and BCAST. The overall methodology behind EADRS, however, is based on the point-to-point communications of TIPC on a local network. Note that while EADRS is indeed similar to TIPC, this is not the absolute method utilized in connection-oriented implementations. The reader should refer to *DECNet Digital Network Architecture Phase IV: NSP Functional Specification* in order to understand the operation of TIPC and how EADRS can be implemented to mimic TIPC.

AA-00-04-00-01-00/0x0660

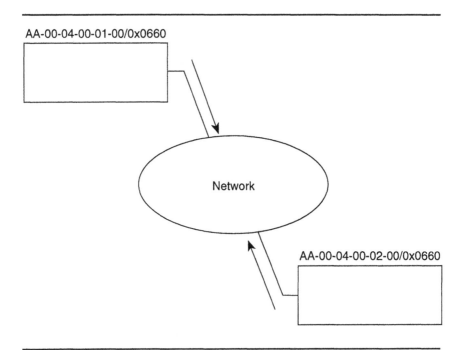

Figure 8.1.   Explicit address configuration.

Figure 8.1 depicts a standard EADRS configuration in its simplest form. This step appears to be backward from BCAST and MCAST; however, this is not the case. In order to implement an EADRS scenario properly, a basic understanding of both connectionless and connection-oriented communications is required. As can be seen, the explicit addresses of the processes are given where each process inherits the address of the respective host node. During a transfer, one process submits information where the packet contains the destination address of the partner process. As can be seen, the protocol is 0x0660, which allows the frame to be received by that node and sent directly to the process that utilizes that protocol. As will be presented, the primary purpose of EADRS is to replace the connection-oriented operations of TIPC with a connectionless implementation. TIPC can exist in a connectionless environment and in some circumstances it is required; however, by incorporating

EADRS into a system, the entire system remains consistent by adhering to the connectionless standard of the system at hand.

PHASES OF EADRS

As with all previously discussed communication methods, there are several phases that should be followed in order to properly establish an explicit addressing scheme. One thing to keep in mind is that EADRS maintains characteristics of both connectionless and connection-oriented communications. By understanding the concepts given in TIPC and MCAST, this chapter should be easy to understand.

Even though EADRS maintains characteristics similar to that of TIPC, there still exists the connectionless problem of communicating with a partner process on the same machine as the primary process. Recall that under TIPC this was possible because a logical link was simply routed back around to the process on that node through the DNA of that node. As with other forms of connectionless communications mentioned, the transmitting process connects below the primary layers of DNA responsible for establishing the logical links to another process. What this means is that, as frames are being transmitted, that transmitting node cannot receive frames at the same time over the same physical device. This leads to the point that a frame sent to another process on the same node must use a higher level of communications such as TIPC.

EADRS Initiation

Since EADRS is connectionless, the process must connect to the node's Ethernet device. This connection establishes a channel that is used for information transfer between the process and the device. As with other forms of connectionless communications, the format for the task specification string is simply the name of the device on the local node. See Table 8.1.

Once the channel to a controller has been returned from the System Service call, the controller's mode must then be set based on the desired operation to be performed. During this setup, a series of parameters are passed to the controller in order to de-

Table 8.1. Device/controller names.

XEA0:	DEUNA and DELUA
XQA0:	DEQNA and DELQA
ETA0:	DEBNA
ESA0:	DESVA

fine the protocol and the size of the I/O buffers and modes as well as a plethora of other functions that can be performed with the controller. For additional information about the available functions that can be defined for the controller, refer to the *VMS I/O User's Reference Manual: Part II* and SYS$LIBRARY:LIB.REQ.

EADRS Transmission

Under TIPC, messages are transferred over a logical link to a destination process. Under MCAST, for example, messages are simply sent out and a receiver process accepts the frame if the protocol and respective addresses match. With EADRS, a frame is sent out onto the network destined for a node, and if a related network process exists on that node, the frame is accepted and given to that process. Under EADRS, the channel is only available between a process and the controller and not between processes. Once the information is passed out of the process along the channel for transmission, the controller performs standard transmission procedures and submits the packet to the network as a frame. One difference between TIPC and EADRS is that the transmit and receive processes do not have to cooperate in order to have information transferred across the network; however, a receive process must exist on the node to which the frame is being directed. The frame is sent by the transmitter process regardless of the state of the receiver process, and it is the responsibility of the receiver process to capture the frame.

EADRS Reception

Once a node receives the frame, the physical layer passes the frame up to the data link layer. The DNA layers then perform the standard address comparisons to see if that frame is destined for the node. If a module exists within that node that accepts the protocol of the packet, the information is passed up to that module, or process, for processing. If no module exists, the frame is not used.

EADRS Termination

In order to terminate an EADRS process, the process may issue a shutdown message to the controller over the channel. Once the call returns, the process should then simply deassign the channel. Recall that in TIPC the primary process and the process located at the other end of the channel should cooperate in the termination; however, since the channel is connected to a device, the device handles its own deassignment with the process on the channel.

IMPLEMENTATION

The EADRS implementation to be presented maintains one process that submits a frame destined for the partner process on the partner node. The code, as will be seen, is similar to MCAST in the methods utilized in transferring the information. With respect to TIPC, this method mimics the ideas presented with logical links in the way that a frame may leave a process and travel to the destination process. For this implementation, the primary process submits frames periodically while the partner process receives and displays the frames.

Primary Process

The primary process is responsible for submitting frames to the network destined for the partner process. As was seen in other connectionless-oriented implementations, the primary process simply establishes a channel to a controller and sets the characteristics of that controller. Because of the similarities to the connectionless-oriented implementations, the defines for the application are identical to the defines for MCAST seen in Figure 6.2 in Chapter 6.

Figure 8.2 contains the extended characteristics buffer, which is utilized in the controller() function of the transmitter. This structure is passed to the controller on startup to notify the device on its required operating characteristics for the channel attached to the process. Note that the characteristics are not shared with other processes/channels and only affect that one channel's characteristics for the process. The buffer is to notify the device that it should preallocate 2 (_BFN) 1500-byte (_BUS) receive buffers where the default is normally 1. This parameter is used to notify the device that it should maintain at least two frames when the process connected to the channel has no read requests queued to the device. Notice also that the padding (_PAD) of the Ethernet packet (_FMT) is disabled, which, as previously stated, allows for data to range from 46 to 1500 bytes with padding performed within the data portion of the frame. The remainder of the buffer maintains information used to register the process with a specific protocol, promiscuous mode state, and so forth.

As can be seen, the process is registered to receive protocol 0x0660 (_PTY); however, there is no structure to register a multicast and/or broadcast address. The address parameter has been eliminated in this instance in order to allow the application to utilize the Ethernet address of the node. Take note here of the

---

```
StartupBuffer =
{
                            /* Setup 2 receive buffers     */
        NMA$C_PCLI_BFN, 2,
                            /* Register for user protocol   */
        NMA$C_PCLI_PTY, 0x0660,
                            /* 1500 byte receive buffer     */
        NMA$C_PCLI_BUS, 1500,
                            /* Frame padding disabled       */
        NMA$C_PCLI_PAD, NMA$C_STATE_OFF,
                            /* Promiscuous disabled         */
        NMA$C_PCLI_PRM, NMA$C_STATE_OFF,
                            /* Ethernet frame format        */
        NMA$C_PCLI_FMT, NMA$C_LINFM_ETH,
                            /* Multicast mode off           */
        NMA$C_PCLI_MLT, NMA$C_STATE_OFF,
};
```

Figure 8.2. Extended characteristics buffer for startup.

states of the promiscuous mode (_PRM) and multicast mode (_MLT) parameters. The state of these parameters depends on the implementation. For this implementation, multicast and promiscuous modes disabled, the process will receive only those packets with a protocol of 0x0660 and the stated destination address of the node. If multicast is enabled, all multicast addresses will be accepted. If promiscuous mode is enabled, any and all packets will be accepted without regard to the protocol and address registered for the process.

Notice in Figure 8.3 that an operation exists that loops through a series of calls to SYS$ASSIGN in an attempt to attach to the device defined in the descriptor and create a channel. Once the channel is created, it is used in a call to SYS$QIOW in order to set up and start the controller for the channel. During the call to SYS$QIOW, the extended characteristics buffer is passed in P2 with functions for IO$_SETMODE and IO$M_STARTUP, which tell the device to start up with the modes specified in P2.

Once the controller is set up, the rest of the functions operate in a manner similar to that of MCAST and every other connectionless implementation introduced. As can be seen in Figure 8.4, two buffers are created for the transmission where one contains the required destination address and protocol and the other contains the data to transfer. In the figure, XMTP5 contains the respective destination Ethernet address in the first 6 bytes, while the last 2 bytes contain the protocol. As can be seen, the protocol value is reversed from the previous declarations (i.e., 0x0660 → 6006) in the extended characteristics buffer. This information is utilized in assigning the information to the outgoing frame's fields for proper routing of the information through the network.

The XMTBUF buffer allows storage of up to 14 bytes for transmission to the destination node's receive process. This buffer was set up for demonstration only and may be extended to the largest data field size of the frame depending on the state of the padding (_PAD) parameter. Now that the buffers are prepared and the data is ready for transmission, the SYS$QIOW function is utilized to transfer the information from the process, down the channel to the device. In the call to SYS$QIOW, the prepared buffers are passed to the function as well as the channel to the device and the

```
struct dsc$descriptor_s devicedescriptor =          /* Device name descriptor     */
          { 0, DSC$K_DTYPE_T, DSC$K_CLASS_S, 0};

                                                    /* Assign the respective device */
for (i=0, status = 0; (status != 1) && (device[i][0] != '*') ; i++)
{
     devicedescriptor.dsc$a_pointer = device[i];
     devicedescriptor.dsc$w_length = strlen(device[i]);
     status = sys$assign(&devicedescriptor, &channel, 0, 0);
}

if (!(status & 1)) lib$stop(status);
     printf("Controller %s\n",device[i-1]);

                                                    /* Start the controller        */
status = sys$qiow(0, channel, IO$_SETMODE + IO$M_STARTUP + IO$M_CTRL,
               iosb, 0, 0, 0, &StartupBufferDescriptor, 0, 0, 0, 0);
```

Figure 8.3.   Controller startup.

```
char  xmtp5[8] = {0xaa,0x00,0x04,0x00,0x58,0x06,0x60,0x06};
char  xmtbuf[14] = {0x00,0x00,0x00,0x00,0x00,0x00,0x00,0x00,
                    0x00,0x00,0x00,0x00,0x00,0x00};

printf("SENDING\n");

                        /* Write using a Wait        */
status = sys$qiow(0, channel, IO$_WRITELBLK, iosb, 0, 0,
                  &xmtbuf[0], sizeof(xmtbuf), 0, 0,
&xmtp5[0], 0);
```

Figure 8.4.   Transmission.

function IO$_WRITELBLK. The device then prepares the information into a legitimate frame and submits it to the physical layer for transmission on the network.

Partner Process

The partner process is responsible for receiving the frames created by the primary process. The definitions for the partner for this implementation are identical to the definitions depicted in Figure 6.2 in Chapter 6 under MCAST. The other characteristic of the partner process identical to the primary process is that of the controller() function utilized to start up the controller on the channel. All calls to the SYS$QIOW System Service function maintain the same buffers and operation as are utilized in the transmitter except for the function specifier.

To receive information from the device, the SYS$QIOW function is called with the IO$_READLBLK function. The received information is then placed into a set of buffers for utilization of the information within the process. As can be seen in Figure 8.5, the P1 buffer of the SYS$QIOW call receives the data field of the

```
status = sys$qiow(0, channel, IO$_READLBLK, iosb, 0, 0,
          &buffer[14], sizeof(buffer)-14, 0, 0, &buffer[0], 0);
```

Figure 8.5.   Reception.

frame. P2 maintains the size of the information required to be retrieved and placed into the buffer of P1. P5 maintains a buffer to capture the header of the frame, specifically the source and destination addresses as well as the protocol of the frame.

EADRS Output

As can be seen in Table 8.2, the first step is to connect a channel to the controller, start up the controller, and set the mode of the controller that can be seen with the Controller: ESA0: output. The next step is to issue a receive request to the controller in order to attempt to receive a frame denoted by RECEIVING followed by Checking and then a frame's header output. As can be seen, the destination address (D) contains the partner process's host node address while the source address (S) of the frame is the address of the primary process's host node. The protocol value of 60- 6 is the value assigned to the frame for transmission to the partner that is registered to receive the said protocol. All of the displayed output is sent from the primary process located on the node designated by the source (S) address of the received frame and is being displayed by the partner process located on the node designated by the destination (D) address.

Table 8.2. Sample output.

```
Controller : ESA0:
QIO Status : 1
RECEIVING
Checking
D: aa 0 4 0 58 6 / S: aa 0 4 0 f6 5 / P: 60- 6
RECEIVING
Checking
D: aa 0 4 0 58 6 / S: aa 0 4 0 f6 5 / P: 60- 6
RECEIVING
Checking
D: aa 0 4 0 58 6 / S: aa 0 4 0 f6 5 / P: 60- 6
RECEIVING
Checking
D: aa 0 4 0 58 6 / S: aa 0 4 0 f6 5 / P: 60- 6
```

PARADIGMS

To maintain consistency with the previous sections of the book, EADRS will be presented with the peer-to-peer and client/server paradigms. The following paradigms will show, as has been shown throughout this chapter, that EADRS maintains similarities between connection-oriented ideas and connectionless-oriented methods. One point to be made here is why EADRS may or may not be used instead of TIPC. The reason for the use of EADRS is that TIPC cannot be seamlessly integrated into applications where MCAST/BCAST communications is being utilized because of the connection-oriented versus connectionless-oriented approaches. It is the characteristics of the implementation's communication requirements that dictate the respective communication requirements.

Peer-to-Peer

A peer-to-peer implementation with EADRS is similar to TIPC in that, essentially, one nodal process communicates with one other nodal process. Either independent process occasionally exchanges a health check message with the partner process on the partner node. The one thing to notice here is that strict adherence to EADRS limits the communication possibilities in such a scenario. In order to communicate with one partner nodal process, one message must be submitted by the primary. Likewise, to communicate with multiple nodes, one message per partner nodal process must be submitted. From prior experience with the previously mentioned methods of communications with respect to redundant messaging and network utilization, it should be deduced that multinodal communication implementations may not be best suited for this type of communication unaccompanied by auxiliary communication methods. One additional note to make is that of the similarities between EADRS and TIPC in the peer-to-peer scenario.

As can be seen in Figure 8.6, there exist two independent systems that perform the same function but operate as redundant backups to each other. In order to maintain a backup scheme such as this, each node must receive and process the information; however, only one node can respond based on the result of the process-

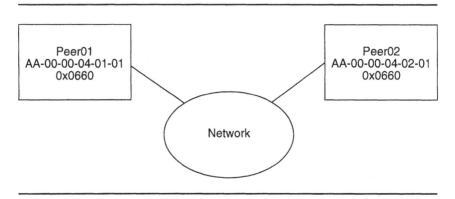

Figure 8.6. Peer-to-peer configuration.

ing. In this instance, both nodes maintain unique addresses based on the Ethernet addresses of the host nodes. When information is destined for an information processor, it will accept the information (based on the protocol and address). Once the information has been processed, a result, based on the specific information, must be sent out onto the network. If both nodes responded simultaneously, there would obviously be increased network utilization, not to mention the confusion at the destination node of the outgoing frame.

Periodically, health checks are performed between the processes. In order to perform this health check, both nodes must perform the check to determine which of the two nodes are active information processors. Let's assume that Peer01 is initially the primary processor. On occasion, the primary node will send a hello message to Peer02 to notify the partner of the primary's state. Once this frame is received by the partner, Peer02 will respond with an acknowledgment message and reset an internal connection timeout timer. If Peer01, the primary, does not respond within the given timeout period, Peer02 assumes that the primary is down and takes control. This control is assumed by first sending a message to Peer01 that the partner is taking control and, in case Peer01 is simply intermittent in performing its health checks, Peer01 should cease primary processor responsibilities. When Peer01 returns, it sends a control message to the partner to notify it that the primary is taking control and that Peer02, the partner, should cease primary processor responsibilities.

Client/Server

When applying EADRS to the client/server (monitor) outlined throughout this book, it is best to combine the methods of MCAST, BCAST, and EADRS together in order to provide a proper explanation of the topic. The reason for this combination is, first, because EADRS alone cannot manage efficient communications in a client/server situation and, second, to show how connectionless communications implementations can be combined into larger, more flexible implementations. One note to make here is that of the evolution of the connectionless model and how it is essentially the same communication subsystem based on different operational characteristics. All connectionless methods can be intermingled in order to properly manage an efficient communication medium between related processes in a system.

The most useful application for EADRS is in a direct messaging situation between clients and servers. What is meant by direct is that a client can send a message directly to a server utilizing the unique address of the host node of the server. The advantage to direct addressing is that of nodal processing for all nodes that do not require the message. As was seen in MCAST, one process can communicate with several nodes while BCAST can, by definition, communicate with all nodes on the local network. Recall from earlier explanations that in order to communicate with one node, a unique MCAST address had to be assigned to each node on the network as well as group-oriented MCAST addresses to related nodes. This unique MCAST address, by definition, was not proper management of communication schemes on the network. By implementing EADRS in addition to MCAST and BCAST, related nodes can, by definition, maintain legitimate group addresses via MCAST and BCAST as well as allowing one-to-one communication via EADRS.

As can be seen in Figure 8.7, a client-aware scenario will be utilized for the explanation because it has characteristics that

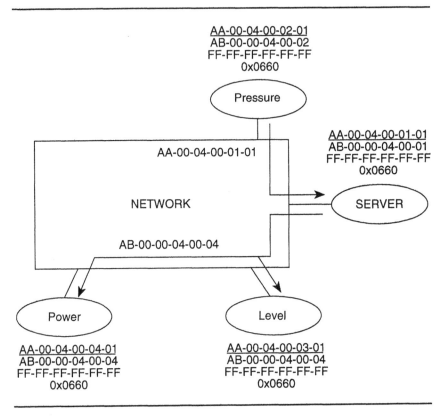

Figure 8.7. Client-aware scenario.

lend themselves to BCAST, MCAST, and EADRS. In the figure there exist three client processes and one server process. The server's responsibility is to gather and maintain data on a centralized node as well as communicate with the clients responsible for monitoring and processing certain types of data. As shown, all nodes maintain a unique address (EADRS), given by the underlined addresses as well as multicast and broadcast addresses. All processes maintain a protocol declaration of 0x0660—the user protocol. From the depiction, the server is communicating with the Power and Level processes which maintain the same multicast address. In a similar manner, the Pressure process is sending a message to the server by means of EADRS to the server's nodal address.

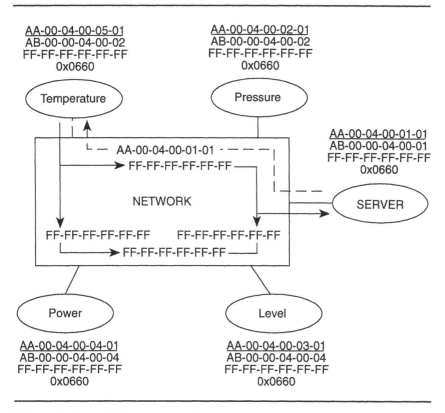

Figure 8.8.   Client aware with new process.

Note that for the first time in this book the reasoning behind the three different implementations of connectionless communications becomes evident in that each process can be communicated within three different manners without any major reconfiguration or modification to any process or implementation. By assigning addresses by definition of the communication method, each process can have unique (EADRS), group (MCAST), and total (BCAST) communications with other related network processes on the network.

Figure 8.8 shows how the system responds to the initialization of a new process that, in this case, is responsible for Temperature values from the server. As can be seen, the Temperature process sends a broadcast out onto the network, which contains the Tem-

FROM NEW PROCESS	RESPONSE FROM SERVER
DEST : FF-FF-FF-FF-FF-FF	DEST : AA-00-04-00-05-01
EADRS : AA-00-04-00-05-01	EADRS : AA-00-04-00-01-01
MCAST : AB-00-00-04-00-02	MCAST : AB-00-00-04-00-01
TOPIC : INIT_MSG	TOPIC : ACK_MSG
TYPE : TEMPERATURE	TYPE : SERVER

Figure 8.9.   Client-aware process initialization messages.

perature process's nodal address, MCAST address, topic, and type. Since all processes on the network can receive the broadcast, a discriminant type must be included to allow special processing on the message. This discriminant type is shown in Figure 8.9 as TOPIC. The reasoning behind this is that the new process, Temperature, does not know which process is the server, but it knows how to open communications with the server. Since, for this example, the server is the only network process that can handle processing of the INIT_MSG topic, the server is the only process that will respond. This method is known as Broadcast Registration in the client-aware scenario, and provides registration of a client process with any server on the network that will listen for and process the initialization broadcast.

Once the server receives the message from the new process, the server stores the node's EADRS and MCAST address information given in the message. The server then uses the EADRS and sends a message back to the new process to notify it of the EADRS and MCAST addresses for the server. The Temperature process then receives the message, processes it, and determines that it is an acknowledgment from the server based on the previous Broadcast Registration request. At this point, the Temperature process is now registered with the server and the server knows that all related Temperature operations and associated data types should be sent to the EADRS of that new process. Likewise, the Temperature process knows that all information

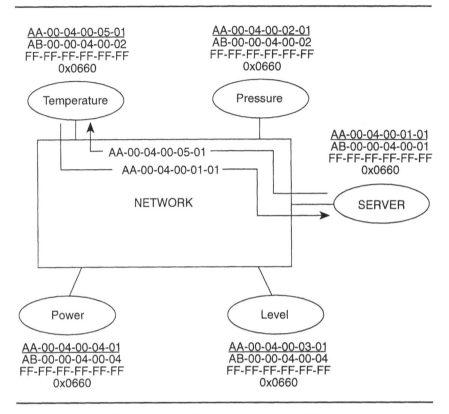

AA-00-04-00-05-01
AB-00-00-04-00-02
FF-FF-FF-FF-FF-FF
0x0660

AA-00-04-00-02-01
AB-00-00-04-00-02
FF-FF-FF-FF-FF-FF
0x0660

Temperature

Pressure

AA-00-04-00-01-01
AB-00-00-04-00-01
FF-FF-FF-FF-FF-FF
0x0660

AA-00-04-00-05-01

AA-00-04-00-01-01

NETWORK

SERVER

Power

Level

AA-00-04-00-04-01
AB-00-00-04-00-04
FF-FF-FF-FF-FF-FF
0x0660

AA-00-04-00-03-01
AB-00-00-04-00-04
FF-FF-FF-FF-FF-FF
0x0660

Figure 8.10.   Client aware after new process initialized.

destined for the server should be sent to the EADRS of the server given in the earlier response from the server.

As can be seen in Figure 8.10, the Temperature process is now part of the overall processing system. Processing can now be easily accomplished between the Temperature process and the server as required by simply submitting a frame destined for the EADRS of the process. A sample message can be seen in Figure 8.11. As shown, the server sends data to the Temperature process containing information that needs to be processed. The client receives the information, processes it, and acknowledges the message back to the server.

FROM SERVER TO TEMPERATURE	FROM TEMPERATURE TO SERVER
DEST : AA-00-04-00-05-01	DEST : AA-00-04-00-01-01
TOPIC : PROC_DATA	TOPIC : ACK_MSG
TYPE : SERVER_TEMP	TYPE : TEMPERATURE
DATA : ...	

Figure 8.11.   Message transfer between server and a client.

SAMPLE EADRS APPLICATION

The two sample applications that follow provide a simple explicit addressing mechanism for testing purposes. The objective is to have a primary process that submits a packet to a partner process on another node. Once the partner receives the frame, the source and destination addresses as well as the protocol are displayed on the screen. This implementation is not as portable as MCAST and BCAST in that the destination address defined in the EADRS_OUT.C writeether() function must be defined to meet the nodal address of the host machine running EADRS_IN.C.

```c
/* EXPLICIT_OUT.C */
#include <descrip.h>                        /* String descriptor types          */
#include <stdio.h>                          /* Standard Input Output header      */
#include <iodef.h>                          /* Input Output definitions          */
#include <string.h>
#include <stdlib.h>

/* Extracted from SYS$LIBRARY:LIB.REQ */
#define NMA$C_PCLI_PTY 2830                 /* Protocol identifier               */
#define NMA$C_PCLI_PRM 2840                 /* Promiscuous mode identifier       */
#define NMA$C_PCLI_BFN 1105                 /* Receive buffer allocation identifier */
#define NMA$C_PCLI_BUS 2801                 /* Respective rcv buffer size        */
#define NMA$C_PCLI_PHA 2820                 /* Port address                      */
#define NMA$C_PCLI_PAD 2842                 /* Frame padding identifier          */
#define NMA$C_PCLI_FMT 2770                 /* Frame format                      */
#define NMA$C_PCLI_MLT 2841                 /* Multicast mode identifier         */
#define NMA$C_PCLI_MCA 2831                 /* Multicast address definition      */

#define NMA$C_STATE_ON 0                    /* State mode enabled                */
#define NMA$C_STATE_OFF 1                   /* State mode disabled               */

#define NMA$C_LINMC_SET 1                   /* Set multicast address             */
#define NMA$C_LINMC_CLR 2                   /* Clear the multicast addresses     */
#define NMA$C_LINMC_CAL 3                   /* Clear all multicast addresses     */

#define NMA$C_LINFM_ETH 1                   /* Ethernet format                   */

int status;
short channel;
```

203

```c
short iosb[4];
unsigned char buffer[1500];

/*-------------------------------------------------------------------
/* controller()
/*-------------------------------------------------------------------
/* Open the ethernet controller.
/*-----------------------------------------------------------------*/
void controller()
{
    char device[5][6] = {"XEA0:", "XQA0:", "ESA0:", "ETA0:", "*"};
    int i, status;

    struct
    {
        short   BFN;
        long    BFN_VAL;
        short   PTY;
        long    PTY_VAL;
        short   BUS;
        long    BUS_VAL;
        short   PAD;
        long    PAD_VAL;
        short   PRM;
        int     PRM_VAL;
        short   ETH;
        long    ETH_VAL;
        short   MLT;
        long    MLT_VAL;
    } StartupBuffer =
```

```
        {
                                            /* Setup 2 receive buffers      */
        NMA$C_PCLI_BFN, 2,
                                            /* Register for user protocol   */
        NMA$C_PCLI_PTY, 0x0660,
                                            /* 1500 byte receive buffer     */
        NMA$C_PCLI_BUS, 1500,
                                            /* Frame padding disabled       */
        NMA$C_PCLI_PAD, NMA$C_STATE_OFF,
                                            /* Promiscuous disabled         */
        NMA$C_PCLI_PRM, NMA$C_STATE_OFF,
                                            /* Ethernet frame format        */
        NMA$C_PCLI_FMT, NMA$C_LINFM_ETH,
                                            /* Multicast mode off           */
        NMA$C_PCLI_MLT, NMA$C_STATE_OFF,
        };

struct
{
        int size;
        int addr;
} StartupBufferDescriptor =
        {
        sizeof(StartupBuffer),    /* Size and address of startup  */
        &StartupBuffer            /* buffer                       */
        };

                                  /* Device name descriptor       */
struct dsc$descriptor_s devicedescriptor =
```

```c
                        { 0, DSC$K_DTYPE_T, DSC$K_CLASS_S, 0};

                               /* Assign the respective device                  */
for (i=0, status = 0; (status != 1) && (device[i][0] != '*') ; i++)
{
    devicedescriptor.dsc$a_pointer = device[i];
    devicedescriptor.dsc$w_length = strlen(device[i]);
    status = sys$assign(&devicedescriptor, &channel, 0, 0);
}

if (!(status & 1)) lib$stop(status);
printf("Controller %s\n",device[i-1]);

                               /* Start the controller                          */
status = sys$qiow(0, channel, IO$_SETMODE + IO$M_STARTUP + IO$M_CTRL,
                 iosb, 0, 0, 0, &StartupBufferDescriptor, 0, 0, 0, 0);

printf("QIO Status : %d\n",status);

if (!(status & 1)) lib$stop(status);
if ((iosb[0] & 1) != 1)
{
    printf("STARTUP ERROR = %d %d %d %d\n",
           iosb[0], iosb[1], iosb[2], iosb[3]);
    printf("             = %2x %2x %2x %2x\n",
           iosb[0], iosb[1], iosb[2], iosb[3]);
    exit(iosb[0]);
}
```

```c
}

/*----------------------------------------------------------------*/
/* writeether()                                                   */
/*----------------------------------------------------------------*/
/* This function writes a packet to the ethernet                  */
/*----------------------------------------------------------------*/
int writeether()
{
    int i;

    char  xmtp5[8] = {0xaa,0x00,0x04,0x00,0x58,0x06,0x60,0x06};  /* Explicit address
    char  xmtbuf[14] = {0x00,0x00,0x00,0x00,0x00,0x00,0x00,0x00,0x00,0x00,
                        0x00,0x00,0x00,0x00,0x00,0x00,0x00,0x00};

    printf("SENDING\n");

                                        /* Write using a Wait
    status = sys$qiow(0, channel, IO$_WRITELBLK, iosb, 0, 0,
                      &xmtbuf[0], sizeof(xmtbuf), 0, 0, &xmtp5[0], 0);

    if (!(status & 1))
    {
        lib$stop(status);
    }

    if (iosb[0] != 1)
    {
```

207

```
            printf("ERROR = %2x %2x %2x %2x\n",
                   iosb[0], iosb[1], iosb[2], iosb[3]);
            lib$stop(iosb[0]);
        }
        return iosb[1] + 14;          /* Return number of bytes transferred          */
}

/*-------------------------------------------------------------------*/
/* main()                                                            */
/*-------------------------------------------------------------------*/
main()
{
        int i;

        controller();
        for (i=0;i<100;i++)
        {
            writeether();
            sleep(5);
        }
}
```

```c
/* EXPLICIT_IN.C*/
#include <descrip.h>                              /* String descriptor types               */
#include <stdio.h>                                /* Standard Input Output header           */
#include <iodef.h>                                /* Input Output definitions               */
#include <string.h>
#include <stdlib.h>

#include "disk02:[edward.library]database.inc"    /* Database functions include file        */

/* Extracted from SYS$LIBRARY:LIB.REQ */
#define NMA$C_PCLI_PTY 2830                        /* Protocol identifier                    */
#define NMA$C_PCLI_PRM 2840                        /* Promiscuous mode identifier            */
#define NMA$C_PCLI_BFN 1105                        /* Receive buffer allocation identifier   */
#define NMA$C_PCLI_BUS 2801                        /* Respective rcv buffer size             */
#define NMA$C_PCLI_PHA 2820                        /* Port address                           */
#define NMA$C_PCLI_PAD 2842                        /* Frame padding identifier               */
#define NMA$C_PCLI_FMT 2770                        /* Frame format                           */
#define NMA$C_PCLI_MLT 2841                        /* Multicast mode identifier              */
#define NMA$C_PCLI_MCA 2831                        /* Multicast address definition           */

#define NMA$C_STATE_ON 0                           /* State mode enabled                     */
#define NMA$C_STATE_OFF 1                          /* State mode disabled                    */

#define NMA$C_LINMC_SET 1                          /* Set multicast address                  */
#define NMA$C_LINMC_CLR 2                          /* Clear the multicast addresses          */
#define NMA$C_LINMC_CAL 3                          /* Clear all multicast addresses          */

#define NMA$C_LINFM_ETH 1                          /* Ethernet format                        */
```

```c
int status;
short channel;
short iosb[4];
unsigned char buffer[1500];

/*------------------------------------------------*/
/* controller()                                   */
/*------------------------------------------------*/
/* Open the ethernet controller.                  */
/*------------------------------------------------*/
void controller()
{
    char device[5][6] = {"XEA0:", "XQA0:", "ESA0:", "ETA0:", "*"};
    int i, stat;

    struct
    {
        short    BFN;
        long     BFN_VAL;
        short    PTY;
        long     PTY_VAL;
        short    BUS;
        long     BUS_VAL;
        short    PAD;
        long     PAD_VAL;
        short    PRM;
        int      PRM_VAL;
        short    ETH;
        long     ETH_VAL;
```

```
        short    MLT;
        long     MLT_VAL;
} StartupBuffer =
    {
                                              /* Setup 2 receive buffers       */
    NMA$C_PCLI_BFN, 2,         /* Register for user protocol    */
    NMA$C_PCLI_PTY, 0x0660,
                               /* 1500 byte receive buffer      */
    NMA$C_PCLI_BUS, 1500,
                               /* Frame padding disabled        */
    NMA$C_PCLI_PAD, NMA$C_STATE_OFF,
                               /* Promiscuous mode disabled     */
    NMA$C_PCLI_PRM, NMA$C_STATE_OFF,
                               /* Ethernet frame format         */
    NMA$C_PCLI_FMT, NMA$C_LINFM_ETH,
                               /* Multicast mode off            */
    NMA$C_PCLI_MLT, NMA$C_STATE_OFF,
    };

struct
    {
    int size;
    int addr;
} StartupBufferDescriptor =
    {
    sizeof(StartupBuffer),     /* Size and address of startup   */
    &StartupBuffer             /* buffer                        */
    };

                                              /* Device name descriptor        */
```

```c
struct dsc$descriptor_s devicedescriptor =
                        { 0, DSC$K_DTYPE_T, DSC$K_CLASS_S, 0};

                        /* Assign the respective device        */
for (i=0, status = 0; (status != 1) && (device[i][0] != '*') ; i++)
{

devicedescriptor.dsc$a_pointer = device[i];
devicedescriptor.dsc$w_length = strlen(device[i]);
status = sys$assign(&devicedescriptor, &channel, 0, 0);

}

if (!(status & 1)) lib$stop(status);
    printf("Controller %s\n",device[i-1]);

                        /* Start the controller                */
status = sys$qiow(0, channel, IO$_SETMODE + IO$M_STARTUP + IO$M_CTRL,
                    iosb, 0, 0, &StartupBufferDescriptor, 0, 0, 0, 0);

printf("QIO Status : %d\n",status);

if (!(status & 1)) lib$stop(status);
if ((iosb[0] & 1) != 1)
{
    printf("STARTUP ERROR = %d %d %d %d\n",
            iosb[0], iosb[1], iosb[2], iosb[3]);
    printf(" = %2x %2x %2x\n",
            iosb[0], iosb[1], iosb[2], iosb[3]);
    exit(iosb[0]);

}

}
```

```c
/*------------------------------------------------------*/
/* checkwriteether()                                    */
/*------------------------------------------------------*/
/* This function simply reads the ethernet controller   */
/*------------------------------------------------------*/
int checkwriteether()
{
    int i;

    printf("RECEIVING\n");
    printf("Checking\n");
    stat = sys$qiow(0, chan, IO$_READLBLK, iosb, 0, 0,
                    &buffer[14], sizeof(buffer)-14, 0, 0, &buffer[0], 0);

                            /* Output the buffer        */
    printf("D: %2x %2x %2x %2x / S: %2x %2x %2x %2x / P: %2x-%2x\n",
           buffer[0],buffer[1],buffer[2],buffer[3],buffer[4],buffer[5],
           buffer[6],buffer[7],buffer[8],buffer[9],buffer[10],buffer[11],
           buffer[12],buffer[13]);

    if (!(stat & 1))
    {
        lib$stop(stat);
    }

    if (iosb[0] != 1)
    {
        printf("ERROR = %2x %2x %2x %2x\n",
               iosb[0], iosb[1], iosb[2], iosb[3]);
```

```
        lib$stop(iosb[0]);
    }
    return iosb[1] + 14;
}

/*------------------------------------------
/* main()
/*------------------------------------------*/
main()
{
    int   i;

    controller();
    for (i=0;i<100;i++)
    {
        checkwriteether();
    }
}
```

9

Implementations and Issues

This chapter will present a series of ideas that can be implemented using the basic ideas presented in this book. We will look at the capability of sharing protocols where multiple processes can use the same protocol on the same node. Protocol sharing was not presented earlier because the idea requires a slightly different approach than was given in the information provided in the earlier sections; however, this section will only provide a basic overview of shared protocols to provide a basic understanding for the reader. Another interesting area to be reviewed is that of the advantages and disadvantages of connection-oriented and connectionless-implementations. The area of routing the frames utilized in a connectionless environment will be covered including a solution to the problem of routing MCAST, BCAST, and EADRS frames. Due to the involved detail required to explain protocol conversion, this topic will be covered in a theoretical, general manner and will show how a protocol converter can be implemented using the methods introduced in this book. An area of current research regarding a compression protocol will be reviewed to allow the reader to see another interesting application for connectionless-implementations. One last topic to be discussed will be that of remote procedure calls (RPC) and how RPCs can be implemented with the information provided. This chapter should be treated as a brainstorming section, since the primary focus of this chapter is simply to provide an overview of different applications that can use the information provided in this book as part of the overall application. Do not take the information provided as the only implementations available, but instead use these as simple examples and theoretical possibilities for implementations for MCAST, BCAST, EADRS, and TIPC.

CONNECTIONLESS OR CONNECTION-ORIENTED

Now that the basic ideas for connectionless and connection-oriented implementations have been presented, the issue of which method to use, and when, should be answered. This issue is important in that under some circumstances connectionless and connection-oriented should be combined to produce an efficient model. Under other circumstances, it is imperative that the implementation be based solely on a connectionless paradigm, while under others, connection-oriented methods are the only solution.

Routing Methods

On a local network, the connectionless-oriented communications methods provided are quite functional; however, these methods cannot be utilized on a wide area network (i.e., across routers) without a little coaxing. In utilizing MCAST or BCAST, the routers do not deal with multidimensional addresses, so these types of transmissions cannot be forwarded to a node at the other end of the circuit. In utilizing EADRS, the standard Ethernet frames discussed in this book do not maintain any related routing information to notify a router that the frame should be forwarded to a node at the other end of the circuit. Essentially, these methods of connectionless communication are limited in a wide area networking environment; however, there are methods available to remedy this situation. The primary method utilized in several cases involves TIPC and network objects known as Guardian Processes.

Guardian Processes provide a means of allowing connectionless communications on local networks while providing connection-oriented intermediate communications to remote

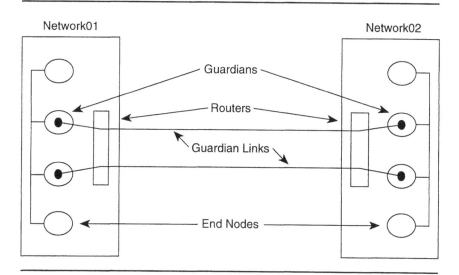

Figure 9.1.   Guardian processes.

nodes on the opposite ends of routers. As can be seen in Figure 9.1, there exist two networks connected by a set of routers. On both networks there also exist two Guardian Processes, which allow for a backup type of scenario in case one of the Guardians should become inactive. In such a situation, connectionless communications may exist on either local network, but, if information needs to be transferred to a node on the remote network, the information is sent by the Guardian located on that network across the logical link to the Guardian located in the other network.

In Figure 9.2, the Guardian Processes shown provide a means of allowing the Guardians to be utilized only if a specific multicast address is intercepted on the network. This type of implementation allows the Guardian to forward only those frames with, in this example, a destination multicast address of AB-00-00-04-01-00 with a protocol of 0x0660. This type of implementation provides for process specific frame mirroring based on the destination, which in turn allows the local connectionless processes to see the remote nodes as being mirrored locally. Put simply, the Guardians act as anchors for remote nodes in that the local processes will be able to

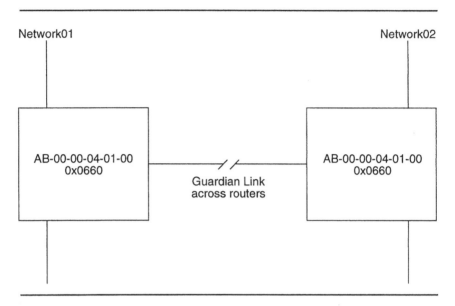

Figure 9.2. Sample Guardian implementation.

have MCAST access to the remote nodes as though they were actually local—by way of the Guardian Processes. At this point, only specific multicast addresses destined for remote nodes are picked up by the local Guardian with that destination multicast address and transferred across the router, via TIPC, to the partner node, which in turn retransmits the frame as a multicast frame on the opposite end.

Recall that multiple MCAST addresses may be registered for one process, which, in this instance, allows for more flexibility in connectionless routing. Figure 9.3 shows a situation that involves multiple MCAST addresses for the local Guardian, while multiple Guardian TIPC links may be established to allow one local process to forward frames across several different routers. This adds the implication that there would exist standard DNA routing mechanisms as well as a secondary routing mechanism specifically for connectionless routing purposes. As shown, the Guardian for Network01 would intercept the multicast-destined frames, reformat

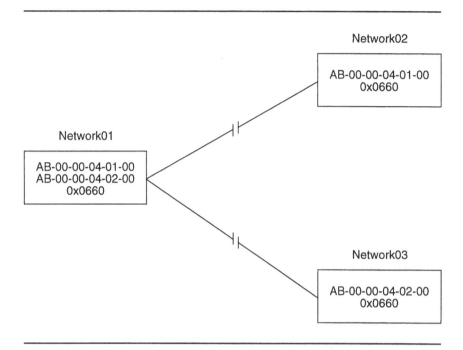

Figure 9.3.   Multipoint Guardian process.

the information from the frame as the data portion of a TIPC transmission, and, based on the last 2 bytes of the multicast address, forward the frame from the link to the remote network for retransmission to that network.

The examples in Figures 9.2 and 9.3 not only apply to MCAST but also may be used for BCAST and EADRS. In BCAST the implementation is straightforward in that the registered address of the Guardian is, of course, FF-FF-FF-FF-FF-FF. Regarding EADRS, this takes things one step further in that the Guardian would perform more of a router emulation than it would for MCAST or BCAST. There are other available methods being researched that will replace the Guardian Processes for EADRS, which take into account the creation of appropriate routing structures for the frame to be routed in a wide area network.

Connection-Oriented versus Connectionless Services

The advantages of connection-oriented services include, for one, the ability to perform error correction at a lower level. In this instance, the DNA maintains the error correction capabilities, which eliminates the need to incorporate a heavy amount of error correction facilities in the network process itself. In a connectionless environment, the network process must maintain some method of error correction internal to the process. The reason for this is that the network process connects below the error-correcting layers of the DNA. This also reveals the fact that a connection-oriented implementation provides for better communication over a noisy line, again, because of the "built in" error correction capabilities.

In a connection-oriented application, a path is available for the life of the logical link, which means that, under normal circumstances, less overhead may be associated with the actual transfer of packets across the network since the resources are already allocated for the communications. This also has a downside in that if no information is being exchanged between the primary and partner processes, this allocation appears to be a waste of valuable resources. In such a case, connectionless would be more conservative with resources since resources are not used unless a frame is being transferred across the network.

In a situation where a connecting circuit may not be stable, causing periodic outages between connecting processes, a connectionless implementation may be better suited. For instance, if a circuit goes down for a connection-oriented application, the link will be lost after the time-out period, forcing a required reestablishment of the link between the processes. In a connectionless implementation, if a circuit should go down, the communicating processes need not reestablish a link but instead can wait for an acknowledgment from the partner. Under minimal schemes, no major link recovery procedures would be required with connectionless as opposed to the link-related recovery schemes required for connection-oriented.

Other interesting differences and complementary functions between connectionless and connection-oriented are in the facts dealing with frame transmissions and network utilization. Take, for instance, a connection-oriented implementation where several processes must communicate with one another. If one process should need to communicate with the other processes, one frame must be sent for each channel connecting each related partner process. Under connectionless, a scheme could easily be devised with MCAST or BCAST to allow one frame to be sent for all related processes. By implementing connectionless in such a situation, the overhead on the network would be reduced considerably.

SERVICE ACCESS POINTS

Service access points (SAPs) can be utilized as an alternative to protocols for process communications. SAPs are also utilized to provide a service entry point for the services of a layer in the layered network hierarchy. In this book, however, the explanation will provide a simple and straightforward explanation of SAP-related information transfer as it applies to connectionless communications. Sample code is provided in Appendix B.

As can be seen in Figure 9.4, instead of registering with a

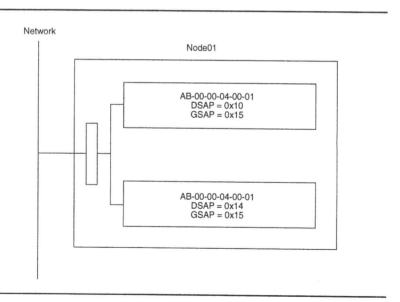

Figure 9.4.   SAP example.

protocol, the processes register with a destination service access point (DSAP), a group service access point (GSAP), and a common destination multicast address. In this circumstance, when an IEEE 802 frame is received for the multicast address, it is routed to the process, or module, with that registered DSAP. As far as the GSAP is concerned, all frames on the network for that multicast address will be forwarded to the processes with the said GSAP.

IEEE 802 Frame Format

Service access point implementations cannot be implemented with the standard Ethernet frame utilized throughout this book; instead, the IEEE 802 frame format must be used. The structure

DESTINATION	Contains the 6-byte destination address of the respective destination that is to receive the packet. May be a multicast, broadcast, or explicit address.
SOURCE	Contains the 6-byte source address of the transmitting node.
LENGTH	The 2-byte length of the 802 frame excluding padding.
DSAP	The 1-byte destination service access point.
SSAP	The 1-byte source service access point.
CTL	A 1- to 2-byte control field.
DATA	A 46- to 1497-byte field for user data for a 1-byte CTL. A 46- to 1496-byte field for user data for a 2-byte CTL field.
CRC	A 32-bit CRC.

Dest	Src	Len	DSAP	SSAP	CTL	Data	CRC

Figure 9.5. IEEE 802 frame.

of this frame is seen in Figure 9.5 and, as shown, is similar to the Ethernet frame except for the fact that the protocol identifier no longer exists. Added to this Ethernet frame are the DSAP, SSAP, and CTL fields to allow other related processing for the data. One other frame to look into, which will not be covered, is the IEEE 802 Extended format, which utilizes a protocol identifier in addition to the given 802 frame.

Starting up the controller is different for the 802 in that there is no entry for a protocol, but instead there exists an entry for the SAP address of the process and the _FMT declaration is no longer _ETH but is instead _802. Receiving an 802 frame is a little different than handling an Ethernet frame. One difference is that the P5 buffer is 16 bytes instead of 14 with the Ethernet frame. Figure 9.6 shows the format of the P5 buffer for the 802 format. Transmitting an 802 frame allows the removal of the protocol values in the P5 buffer, but the CTL and DSAP must be added into the P4 parameter of the SYS$QIO[W] function. To provide the CTL and DSAP information, a simple descriptor is utilized, as depicted in Figure 9.7.

DESTINATION	6-byte destination address
SOURCE	6-byte source address
DSAP	1-byte destination service access point
SSAP	1-byte source service access point
CTL	1- or 2-byte control

Figure 9.6. IEEE 802 P5 buffer.

SIZE	4-byte length value of the CTL and DSAP information
DSAP	1-byte destination service access point
CTL	2-byte control

Figure 9.7. IEEE 802 P4 buffer.

SAP Definitions

As stated earlier, a SAP is a service access point, which is an entry point into a module, or layer, to provide servicing to requesting network entities. There are several different implementations of SAPs that can be utilized in different ways to perform different actions. Some of these implementations include SSAPs, DSAPs, and GSAPs.

SSAPs. SSAPs are source service access points and represent the source process's SAP from which the frame originated. SSAPs are designated by a zero in the low-order bit for commands and a 1 for responses. If the low-order bit is zero, the CTL field of the IEEE 802 frame may contain the commands outlined in Table 9.1.

DSAPs. DSAPs are destination service access points and represent the module, or process, for which the frame is destined. The DSAP may represent an individual DSAP by a zero in the low-order bit, or may represent a GSAP with a 1 in the low-order bit. DSAPs must be unique per channel on a controller, but GSAPs may be duplicated to allow the sharing of information between processes. In such a situation, frames coming into the controller may be multiplexed between all processes with the same GSAP. For flexibility in grouping network-oriented processes on a machine, up to four GSAPs may be designated per process.

Table 9.1.   SSAP commands.

NMA$C_CTLVL_UI	Used in the CTL field to notify the receiver that the frame contains user data.
NMA$C_CTLVL_XID NMA$C_CTLVL_XID_P	Used to exchange information about a port. _XID_P represents a **1** poll while _XID represents a **0** poll. This is also utilized in a response to the respective information poll.
NMA$C_CTLVL_TEST NMA$C_CTLVL_TEST_P	Used to test a connection and may be sent as a _TEST_P for a **1** poll or a **0** poll. This is also utilized in a response to the respective information poll.

PROTOCOL SHARING

Protocol sharing allows a set of processes to share the same protocol with the requirement that the destination addresses for the respective channels are different across all channels sharing a protocol. Recall the earlier discussion that the primary reason that protocols could not be shared between processes on the node was the problem with multiplexing frames between network processes on a node. This situation is overcome by the fact that when a protocol is established as shareable, it can be utilized between network processes with different destination-explicit addresses. This eliminates that problem of multiplexing packets since, even though the protocols are the same, the difference in their destination addresses allows for appropriate packet routing. In order to accomplish this, there are a few entries in the characteristics buffer that must be established that are different than the previous implementations.

As is shown in Figure 9.8, the protocol type is the user protocol that has been used for other applications outlined, while (not shown) the frame format is the standard Ethernet frame format. The frame format must be the Ethernet frame for this type of

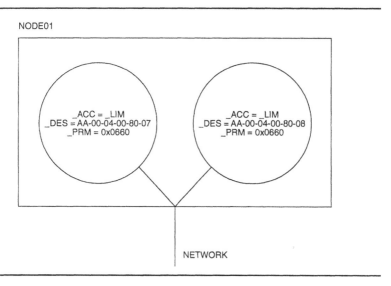

NODE01

_ACC = _LIM
_DES = AA-00-04-00-80-07
_PRM = 0x0660

_ACC = _LIM
_DES = AA-00-04-00-80-08
_PRM = 0x0660

NETWORK

Figure 9.8.   Shared protocol configuration.

implementation since, for example, a protocol identifier is not utilized with the previously mentioned 802 frame. The _DES identifier passed in the characteristics buffer is a counted string identifying the explicit address for the process. In this implementation, the _DES identifier cannot be a multicast address but must be a standard software, or nodal, address. This identifier is only applicable if the protocol access mode, _ACC, is set to the limited access/shared with destination identifier, _LIM. As can be seen, any frame that arrives at the node with a protocol of 0x0660 is utilized and passed to the process with the matching destination address.

PROTOCOL CONVERSION

Protocol conversion is a method of protocol manipulation that is currently implemented by a number of vendors. Some conversion implementations allow conversion between TCP/IP and DECNet, TCP/IP and SNA, and a plethora of other conversion methods for other protocols available. Currently, an area of research has opened up to use the previously mentioned methods of process communication for protocol conversion-related implementations. This section will not detail the concepts of protocol conversion, but will instead show some interesting methods concerning how the information provided in this book can be utilized for protocol-related implementations.

Take a simple example where NODE01 communicates primarily by the Internet protocol and where NODE02 communicates via DECNet. Under certain circumstances, NODE01 would need to communicate with NODE02. In order for this to be accomplished, some method must be designed that allows NODE01 to send an IP frame to an intermediate node and have it converted to a DECNet Phase IV frame for acceptance by NODE02. This is the long way around to reach a conversion solution, but the detail provided will give a basic understanding of the method.

As can be seen in Figure 9.9, NODE01 transmits an IP frame while NODE02 receives all Phase IV-related frames. The INODE provides an intermediate conversion to intercept IP frames, extract the destination address and related data, and pass the information to the Phase IV process, which in turn transmits the

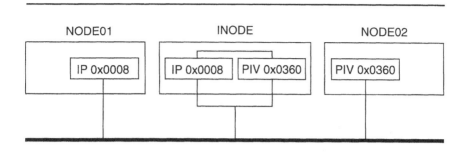

Figure 9.9.   Example of protocol conversion implementation.

frame to NODE02 as a Phase IV-related frame. With regard to the information in this book, the idea behind this type of implementation is quite straightforward. Recall that a process can be registered to receive certain frames based on the _PTY field of the characteristics buffer required for controller startup. In this instance, the INODE processes insert their protocol identifiers into the _PTY field and register on the node. The network processes will then activate only when a related frame exists on the network with that specific protocol identifier in the protocol field of the frame. Internal to the two processes are the protocol-specific functions that allow for conversion of the information from one protocol to another as required.

COMPRESSION PROTOCOL

The compression protocol to be outlined is an area of research that is currently under way. The primary purpose of this type of protocol implementation is to provide a means of transferring large amounts of information with less network overhead as well as in a shorter amount of time. This is an area of interest for the author and could provide some interesting results as the research progresses. In its most basic form, the idea involves compressing a file and transferring the information to a destination node. Once at the destination node, the information would be uncompressed and stored for use on that node. Needless to say there are more implementations in store for a completed version, but this document will not go beyond the basic ideas covered earlier.

There will exist on the originating node a network process that maintains a compression algorithm, a means of receiving input for file transfer commands, and a network connection. The compression algorithm can, for this example, be any efficient algorithm that provides for a compact and encapsulated set of information in one structure. The input mechanism for this example is a simple logical definition containing the name of the file to copy to a remote node. The network connection is a simple EADRS implementation that allows for the transfer of the information, based on protocol, to a destination node.

As can be seen in Figure 9.10, NODE01 maintains the compression algorithm and the file to transfer. The process is connected to the network utilizing the _PTY identifier 0x0660, which has been chosen for example only. This protocol identifier would be best chosen based on a unique value that will probably not be duplicated across the system. The information is compressed and submitted to the network destined for NODE02 with

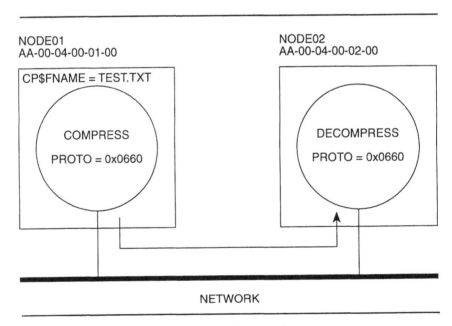

Figure 9.10. Compression protocol example.

SEQ	The sequence number for the current frame
TOTAL	The total number of frames associated with the data being transferred
DATA	The actual compressed data block

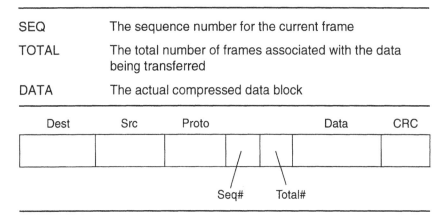

Figure 9.11.   Ethernet frame with sequencing.

the said protocol. Once NODE02 receives the information, it decompresses the data and stores it on the node.

Note here how information that exceeds 1500 bytes is handled, which, as you should recall, is the maximum size that an Ethernet frame can handle. In such a situation the information would have to be maintained in such a way that it can be compressed and transferred in discrete blocks that will fit into the Ethernet frame format. Each frame would have to be marked with sequence numbers as well as the total number of blocks that will be transferred.

As can be seen in Figure 9.11, the data portion of the Ethernet frame is a structure that contains a byte value for the current sequence number and a byte value for the total number of frames associated with the current file being transferred. Part of the sequence structure is the actual compressed data associated with the respective sequence number. What can be accomplished here is error correction and segmented transfer sequencing. For instance, as the information is transferred, the blocks are uncompressed and appended to the destination file. If, for one sequence number, an error should occur during the uncompress stage, the receiver could send the errored sequence number back to the transmitter to have the transmitter resend that block.

Again, this is part of an area of research but provides a viable protocol implementation for transferring vast amounts of information. One of the possible drawbacks to this scenario is the time it may take to compress/decompress a block of information. In the time it takes to handle the information, could that information have already been sent and received? However, the idea behind this section was to provide direction for future research as well as provide the reader with another possible implementation for the information provided in this book.

REMOTE PROCEDURE CALLS

In a single process, a procedure (i.e., function) call is a method used for transferring control from one part of a process to another to perform a specific function for the process as a whole. When such a call is made, there exists a transfer of information known as parameters followed, usually, by a return value as a result of the function call. These types of calls are known as local procedure calls and are linked into the process at link time. In a process implementing remote procedure calls, a process calls to a procedure (function) located in a remote process on a remote node. In such a circumstance, a remote procedure call allows a process to call a procedure, passing the required parameters and receiving the return value in a seamless fashion located on the other node. These RPC functions are "linked" at runtime and, as stated, are available to a process via interprocess communications in a fashion that allows that procedure to appear to exist on the local node.

As this applies to DECNet Phase IV, there are no immediate functions available for RPCs; however, DECNet Phase V does maintain a facility for RPCs as part of the distributed computing services. Under Phase IV, RPC emulation is possible by means of the interprocess communication capabilities provided in this book. This section will provide a brief outline for RPC application development as it applies to the connectionless implementations described earlier. Regarding connection-oriented applications, this section will be presented as generically as possible to provide for comparisons by the reader between possible communication implementations.

RPC Entities

There are two primary entities required for remote procedure calls. The first is the RPC Server, which maintains the procedures (functions) accessed by remote calling processes. The other is an RPC Client, which calls the RPCs maintained by the Server. For this type of situation to exist, some method of interprocess communications must exist to allow the two entities to communicate so that the RPC requests and acknowledgments can be executed.

In order to execute an RPC, the client process calls a local procedure in the client stub. The client stub then takes the passed information and appropriately formats the information for submission to the RPC Server. The formatted information is then sent to the RPC Server over the network for call processing whether the communications be connectionless or connection-oriented. Within the RPC Server, the server stub stands waiting for a procedure call submission from the network. The server stub receives the previously submitted call and converts the received information to call a server function with the arguments received. Once the respective call is complete, the server stub returns the return value(s) back to the client stub over the network. Once the client stub receives this return information, it submits the data to the main portion of the client process, which in turn resumes normal processing as if the previous call was made to a local function.

RPC Configurations

For ease of explanation, a client/server implementation will be utilized. One reason for this approach is because throughout this book we have stayed with this paradigm and it would be easier to discuss such an implementation based on known facts. The other reason is due to the fact that an RPC implementation is suited quite well to the client/server paradigms provided earlier. For this explanation we will start with the server process and explain how the implementation registers functions to prepare for remote calls followed by an explanation of how the client actually performs these calls. This explanation will be provided from a generic, conceptual standpoint with references to the information provided earlier. See Figure 9.12.

RPC Server. The RPC Server process is the process that maintains the calls to be accessed by remote clients. One primary requirement for allowing external processes to call to server

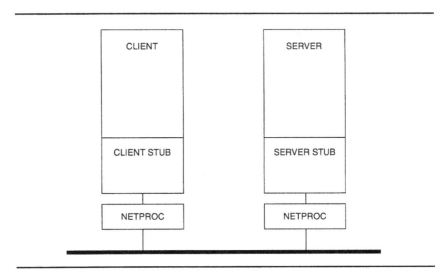

Figure 9.12. RPC client/server configuration.

functions is to provide a means of allowing the server to locate the function by some type of tagname. In this instance, the server will register the names of the desired functions in a list based on a function tagname and a pointer to the actual function. For instance, as can be seen in Figure 9.13, there exists a function called AddNumbers() that has been written into the server. In order to register the function, the server maintains a call to RegisterRPCFunc(), which passes a tagname, parameter types, and a pointer to the function AddNumbers(). Notice in the call to RegisterRPCFunc() that the last two parameters represent two integer values in the order in which they are passed to the registered function. This portion of the parameter line should be a variable-length argument list in order to accommodate different parameter types, and parameter count, for the registered function's parameter list.

The call to RegisterRPCFunc() accepts the information passed in the parameter line and stores the information in a list structure, as is shown in Figure 9.14. As can be seen, the tagname, pointer to the associated function, and the parameter types are all stored for future reference when the client makes an RPC request.

```
int AddNumbers(int A, int B)
{
    return(A+B);
}
.
.
.
main()
    { RegisterRPCFunc("ADDNUM", AddNumbers,I,I,I);
.
.
.
}
```

Figure 9.13.   Registering an RPC function.

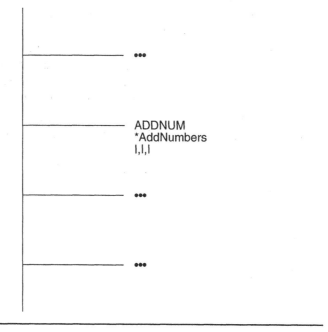

ADDNUM
*AddNumbers
I,I,I

Figure 9.14.   RPC function list.

```
RPCRequest(retval,retlen,"ADDNUM",(int)10,(int)20);
```

Figure 9.15. Calling an RPC function.

The first field, ADDNUM, is the tagname reference, while the second field, AddNumbers, is a pointer to the function. The final field in the entry includes the parameters used to return information from and pass information to the function. The three I's in this instance represent integer values. The first I is the return value for the function, while the next two I's are the values passed to the function.

RPC Client. The RPC Client maintains a local call to the client stub, which allows calls to be formatted and transferred to the server. As is shown in Figure 9.15, there exists a function named RPCRequest() that allows the user to make a request to the remote RPC Server. Note that this call resides in the client stub and is called from the client primary functions. As can be seen, the RPCRequest() passes the tagname of the function, located in the remote server, as well as the parameters to be passed to respective remote function. The return value of the remote procedure is passed as a void pointer in the retval parameter along with the length of the retval stored in retlen. It is the responsibility of the client process to unpack the information stored in retval based on retlen and handle processing accordingly. As can be

```
int AddNumbers(int A, int B)
{
    int retval;
    int retlen;

    RPCRequest((int)retval,(int)retlen,"ADDNUM",(int)A,
        (int)B);

    return(retval);
}
```

Figure 9.16. Client function.

seen, the RPCRequest() function should also utilize a variable-length argument list for the parameters to be passed to the function for the tagname.

To simplify the call, a separate function can be created that allows seamless integration of the operation within the client. As can be seen in Figure 9.16, there exists a function with the same name, AddNumbers(), as that of the server. This allows the client to call the function AddNumbers() in order to provide, a seamless integration of the function. This function then, in turn, appropriately formats the information for the call to the RPCRequest() function.

Execution. Performing a client request is quite simple now that the basic registration and calls have been established. At this point, the discussion has to drop to a lower level in order to demonstrate how the respective call, or request, is acknowledged. The call to RPCRequest() allows the client stub to create a frame destined for the server stub. This frame maintains the standard information required for frame routing as well as an RPC-related structure in the data portion of the frame containing the function tagname and parameters. Once the server stub receives this frame, it takes the tagname from the passed RPC structure and locates that tagname in the RPC function list mentioned earlier. Once the tagname is located, the function pointer is utilized to pass the parameters given in the RPC structure to that function in the format provided in the RPC function list.

After the call has completed, the server stub formats the return value for return to the calling client stub. The client stub receives this information, extracts the return value, and passes it as a return parameter of the RPCRequest() function. If a return value is expected, the RPCRequest() function will utilize a wait operation to halt processing until the function returns; otherwise, the RPCRequest() simply issues the request and continues processing.

Communications. Communications is handled by the respective stubs of the client and the server. As seen in Figure 9.17, this implementation can utilize the anonymous client paradigm for MCAST. As is shown, there are multiple clients and one server

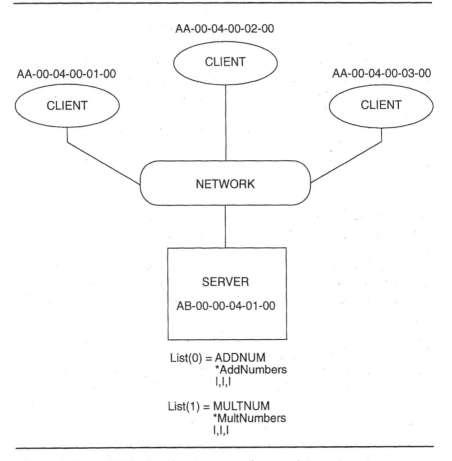

Figure 9.17. RPC client/server example.

where the server does not know of the clients in an immediate fashion, while the clients do not know where the server is located. Each client maintains a protocol of, again, 0x0660 as well as the nodal address of the respective host node (EADRS). The server maintains a multicast address to allow access by the clients regardless of the nodal address of the server.

When a client stub makes an RPCRequest() to the server stub, it creates an Ethernet frame with a destination address of AB-00-00-04-01-00 and a protocol of 0x0660. The server stub extracts the source address from the frame in order to return the return value of the called function. As can be seen, the configuration provides for the fact that the clients and the server do not have to know about each other until a call to a function is required. All clients know, however, that the server can be reached by the multicast address of AB-00-00-04-01-00, but the client does not have to know the explicit address of the server. In this instance, the server can be anywhere and reply to the client. In the reply to the client, the server knows the client's address for the reply only to get the reply back to the requesting client. This return address is supplied by the source address in the client's request Ethernet frame.

Partial Protocol Listing

The following brief table of protocol values was acquired through discussions regarding protocol types that appear on an Ethernet. The values in the Hex column are utilized in the _PTY field of the extended characteristics buffer passed to a controller on startup.

Hex	Description
0x0008	DoD Internet Protocol
0x000A	Xerox 802.3
0x003C	NetBios Protocol
0x0090	DEC Loopback Test Protocol
0x0290	TCP/IP System Management (Bridge Comm)
0x0360	DECNet
0x0460	Lat Protocol
0x0660	DEC User Protocol
0x3781	Novell Netware
0x9B80	Appletalk
0xD580	IBM SNA over Ethernet

Service Access Point Source Code

The following code represents the use of Service Access Points. The samples implement a MCAST type of configuration that is only for demonstration purposes.

SSAP-DSAP_OUT.C sends out three frames with different DSAPs. The first frame is destined for SAP 0x10, the second goes to SAP 0x14, and the third goes to 0x15. Notice that the first two are specific SAPs since the low-order bit is zero. The third is a GSAP since the low-order bit is a 1. The second 2 bytes in the control structure (ctlstructx) are the 2-byte control code sent to the remote process representing NMA$C_CTLVL_UI. The frames are also destined for an MCAST address of AB-00-00-04-00-01.

SSAP-DSAP_IN.C registers itself with a DSAP of 0x10, GSAP of 0x15, and an MCAST of AB-00-00-04-00-01. Any 802 frames that travel on the network with these parameters are received by the process and printed to SYS$OUTPUT.

```c
/*SSAP-DSAP_OUT.C*/
#include <descrip.h>          /* String descriptor types            */
#include <stdio.h>            /* Standard Input Output header       */
#include <iodef.h>            /* Input Output definitions           */
#include <string.h>

#define NMA$C_PCLI_PTY 2830   /* Protocol ID                        */
#define NMA$C_PCLI_PRM 2840   /* Promiscuous mode                   */
#define NMA$C_PCLI_BFN 1105   /* Number of receive buffers          */
#define NMA$C_PCLI_BUS 2801   /* Receive buffer size                */
#define NMA$C_PCLI_FMT 2770   /* Frame format                       */
#define NMA$C_PCLI_GSP 2773   /* Group Service Point                */
#define NMA$C_PCLI_SAP 2772   /* Service Access Point               */
#define NMA$C_PCLI_PID 2774   /* Protocol ID                        */
#define NMA$C_PCLI_SRV 2771   /* Class I Service                    */

#define NMA$C_STATE_ON 0      /* Mode enabled                       */
#define NMA$C_STATE_OFF 1     /* Mode disabled                      */

#define NMA$C_LINMC_SET 1     /* Set PHA                            */
#define NMA$C_LINMC_CLR 2     /* Clear PHA                          */
#define NMA$C_LINMC_SDF 4     /* set PHA to default decnet          */
#define NMA$C_LINSR_CLI 2
/*     NMA$C_CTLVL_UI         NMA$C_CTLVL_XID_P      NMA$C_CTLVL_XID */
/*     NMA$C_CTLVL_TEST_P     NMA$C_CTLVL_TEST                      */
/*     (Used for the U field of the 802 frame only)                */

#define NMA$C_LINFM_802E 0
#define NMA$C_LINFM_ETH 1
#define NMA$C_LINFM_802 2
```

```c
int status;
short channel;
short iosb[4];
unsigned char buf[1500];

/*---------------------------------------------------------------------------
/* controller()
/*---------------------------------------------------------------------------
/* Open the ethernet controller and set the characteristics.
/*-------------------------------------------------------------------------*/
void controller()
{
    char device[5][6] = {"XEA0:", "XQA0:", "ESA0:", "ETA0:", "*"};
    int i, stat;

    struct
    {
        short   BFN;
        long    BFN_VAL;
        short   BUS;
        long    BUS_VAL;
        short   ETH;
        long    ETH_VAL;
        short   SAP;
        long    SAP_VAL;
        short   PRM;
        long    PRM_VAL;
        short   SRV;
        long    SRV_VAL;
        short   GSP;
        long    GSP_VAL;
```

```c
} StartupBuffer =
    {
                /* Number of receive buffers      */
    NMA$C_PCLI_BFN, 2,
                /* Size of receive buffers        */
    NMA$C_PCLI_BUS, 1500,
                /* IEEE 802 frame format          */
    NMA$C_PCLI_FMT, NMA$C_LINFM_802,
                /* Service access point for this process */
    NMA$C_PCLI_SAP, (long)0x10,
                /* Promiscuous mode off           */
    NMA$C_PCLI_PRM, NMA$C_STATE_OFF,
                /* Class I service                */
    NMA$C_PCLI_SRV, NMA$C_LINSR_CLI,
                /* Group service access point     */
    NMA$C_PCLI_GSP, (long)0x11
    };

struct
{
    int size;
    int addr;
} StartupBufferDesscriptor =
    {
    sizeof(StartupBuffer), &StartupBuffer
    };

struct dsc$descriptor_s devicedescriptor = { 0, DSC$K_DTYPE_T, DSC$K_CLASS_S, 0};

for (i=0, stat = 0; (stat != 1) && (dev[i][0] != '*') ; i++)
```

```c
    {
      devicedescriptor.dsc$a_pointer = device[i];
      devicedescriptor.dsc$w_length = strlen(device[i]);
      status = sys$assign(&devicedescriptor, &channel, 0, 0);

      if (!(status & 1)) lib$stop(status);
      printf("Using ethernet controller %s\n",device[i-1]);

      status = sys$qiow(0, channel, IO$_SETMODE + IO$M_STARTUP + IO$M_CTRL,iosb, 0, 0, 0,
                        &StartupBufferDescriptor, 0, 0, 0, 0);

      if (!(status & 1)) lib$stop(status);
      if ((iosb[0] & 1) != 1)
        {
          printf("ERROR : %d %d %d %d\n",iosb[0], iosb[1], iosb[2], iosb[3]);
          exit(iosb[0]);
        }
    }

/*---------------------------------------------------------------------*/
/* writeether()                                                        */
/*---------------------------------------------------------------------*/
/* This function writes a packet to the ethernet                       */
/*---------------------------------------------------------------------*/
int writeether()
{
    int    i;                              /* Destination multicast address   */
```

245

```
char    xmtp5[6] = {0xab,0x00,0x00,0x04,0x00,0x01};
char    xmtbuf[14] = {0x00,0x00,0x00,0x02,0x00,
                      0xaa,0x00,0x00,0x04,0x00,0x58,0x06,
                      0x00,0x00,0x00,0x00,0x00};

struct
{
    int    sizeofstruct;
    int    adrsofstruct;
}tempstruct;

                            /* DSAP,CTL    */
char    ctlstruct1[3] = {0x10,0x03,0x00};          /* DSAP 1*/
char    ctlstruct2[3] = {0x14,0x03,0x00};          /* DSAP 2*/
char    ctlstruct3[3] = {0x15,0x03,0x00};          /* GSAP 1*/

printf("SENDING\n");              /* Send to GSAP 1 named in ctlstruct3      */

tempstruct.sizeofstruct=3;
tempstruct.adrsofstruct= &ctlstruct3;
status = sys$qiow(0, channel, IO$_WRITELBLK, iosb, 0, 0,
                  &xmtbuf[0], sizeof(xmtbuf), 0, &tempstruct, &xmtp5[0], 0);

                                  /* Send to DSAP 1 named in ctlstruct1      */

tempstruct.sizeofstruct=3;
tempstruct.adrsofstruct= &ctlstruct1;
status = sys$qiow(0, channel, IO$_WRITELBLK, iosb, 0, 0,
                  &xmtbuf[0], sizeof(xmtbuf), 0, &tempstruct, &xmtp5[0], 0);

                                  /* Send to SSAP 2 named in ctlstruct2      */

tempstruct.sizeofstruct=3;
tempstruct.adrsofstruct= &ctlstruct2;
```

```c
    status = sys$qiow(0, channel, IO$_WRITELBLK, iosb, 0, 0,
                &xmtbuf[0], sizeof(xmtbuf), 0, &tempstruct, &xmtp5[0], 0);
    if (!(status & 1))
    {
            lib$stop(status);
    }

    if (iosb[0] != 1)
    {
            fprintf(stderr, "ERROR : %d %d %d %d\n", iosb[0], iosb[1], iosb[2], iosb[3]);
            lib$stop(iosb[0]);
    }

    return iosb[1] + 14;            /* return byte count */
}

/*----------------------------------------------------------------*/
/* main()
/*----------------------------------------------------------------*/
main()
{
    int i,j;
    unsigned int packets;

    controller();
    for (i=0;i<100;i++)
    {
            writeether();
            sleep(5);
    }
}
```

```
/*SSAP-DSAP_IN.C*/
#include <descrip.h>        /* String descriptor types              */
#include <stdio.h>          /* Standard Input Output header         */
#include <iodef.h>          /* Input Output definitions             */
#include <string.h>

#define NMA$C_PCLI_PTY 2830     /* Protocol                         */
#define NMA$C_PCLI_PRM 2840     /* Promiscuous mode                 */
#define NMA$C_PCLI_BFN 1105     /* Number of receive buffers        */
#define NMA$C_PCLI_BUS 2801     /* Receive buffer size              */
#define NMA$C_PCLI_FMT 2770     /* Frame format                     */
#define NMA$C_PCLI_GSP 2773     /* Group Service Point              */
#define NMA$C_PCLI_SAP 2772     /* Service Access Point             */
#define NMA$C_PCLI_PID 2774     /* Protocol ID                      */
#define NMA$C_PCLI_SRV 2771     /* Class I Service                  */

#define NMA$C_STATE_ON 0        /* Mode enabled                     */
#define NMA$C_STATE_OFF 1       /* Mode disabled                    */

#define NMA$C_LINMC_SET 1       /* Set PHA                          */
#define NMA$C_LINMC_CLR 2       /* Clear PHA                        */
#define NMA$C_LINMC_SDF 4       /* set PHA to default decnet        */

#define NMA$C_LINSR_CLI 2
/*    NMA$C_CTLVL_UI        NMA$C_CTLVL_XID_P      NMA$C_CTLVL_XID  */
/*    NMA$C_CTLVL_TEST_P    NMA$C_CTLVL_TEST                       */
/*    (Used for the U field of the 802 frame only)
*/
```

```c
#define NMA$C_LINFM_802E  0
#define NMA$C_LINFM_ETH   1
#define NMA$C_LINFM_802   2

int status;
short channel;
short iosb[4];
unsigned char buf[1500];

/*-------------------------------------------------------------------
/* controller()
/*-------------------------------------------------------------------
/* Open the ethernet controller and set the characteristics.
/*-------------------------------------------------------------*/
void controller()
{
    char device[5][6] = {"XEA0:", "XQA0:", "ESA0:", "ETA0:", "*"};
    int i, stat;

    struct
    {
        short  BFN;
        long   BFN_VAL;
        short  BUS;
        long   BUS_VAL;
        short  ETH;
        long   ETH_VAL;
        short  SAP;
        long   SAP_VAL;
        short  PRM;
```

```
        long    PRM_VAL;
        short   SRV;
        long    SRV_VAL;
        short   GSP;
        long    GSP_VAL;
} StartupBuffer =
{
                                /* Number of receive buffers             */
        NMA$C_PCLI_BFN, 2,
                                /* Size of receive buffers               */
        NMA$C_PCLI_BUS, 1500,
                                /* IEEE 802 frame format                 */
        NMA$C_PCLI_FMT, NMA$C_LINFM_802,
                                /* Service access point for this process */
        NMA$C_PCLI_SAP, (long)0x10,
                                /* Promiscuous mode off                  */
        NMA$C_PCLI_PRM, NMA$C_STATE_OFF,
                                /* Class I service                       */
        NMA$C_PCLI_SRV, NMA$C_LINSR_CLI,
                                /* Group service access point            */
        NMA$C_PCLI_GSP, (long)0x15,
                                /* Multicast address                     */
        NMA$C_PCLI_MCA, 8, NMA$C_LINMC_SET,
        0xab,0x00,0x00,0x04,0x00,0x01
};

struct
{
        int size;
        int addr;
```

```c
} StartupBufferDesscriptor =
    {
        sizeof(StartupBuffer), &StartupBuffer
    };

struct dsc$descriptor_s devicedescriptor = { 0, DSC$K_DTYPE_T, DSC$K_CLASS_S, 0};

for (i=0, stat = 0; (stat != 1) && (dev[i][0] != '*') ; i++)
{
    devicedescriptor.dsc$a_pointer = device[i];
    devicedescriptor.dsc$w_length = strlen(device[i]);
    status = sys$assign(&devicedescriptor, &channel, 0, 0);
}

if (!(status & 1)) lib$stop(status);
printf("Using ethernet controller %s\n",device[i-1]);

status = sys$qiow(0, channel, IO$_SETMODE + IO$M_STARTUP + IO$M_CTRL,iosb, 0, 0, 0,
    &StartupBufferDescriptor, 0, 0, 0, 0);

if (!(status & 1)) lib$stop(status);
if ((iosb[0] & 1) != 1)
{
    printf("ERROR : %d %d %d\n",iosb[0], iosb[1], iosb[2], iosb[3]);
    exit(iosb[0]);
}
```

```
/*---------------------------------------------------------------*/
/* checkwriteether()                                             */
/*---------------------------------------------------------------*/
/* Read a packet from the network.                               */
/*---------------------------------------------------------------*/
int checkwriteether()
{
    int    i;

    printf("RECEIVING\n");
    printf("Checking\n");
    status = sys$qiow(0, channel, IO$_READLBLK, iosb, 0, 0,
                      &buf[15], sizeof(buf)-15, 0, 0, &buf[0], 0);

    printf("D:%2x%2x%2x%2x%2x/S:%2x%2x%2x%2x%2x%2x/DSP:%2x SSP:%2x CTL:%2x\n",
           buf[0],buf[1],buf[2],buf[3],buf[4],buf[5],
           buf[6],buf[7],buf[8],buf[9],buf[10],buf[11],buf[12],buf[13],buf[14]);

    if (!(stat & 1))
    {
        lib$stop(status);
    }

    if (iosb[0] != 1)
    {
        fprintf(stderr, "ERROR : %d %d %d\n", iosb[0], iosb[1], iosb[2], iosb[3]);
        lib$stop(iosb[0]);
    }
    return iosb[1] + 14;                    /* return byte count */
}
```

```
/*-----------------------------------------------------------------------
/* main()
/*-----------------------------------------------------------------*/
main()
{
    int i,j;
    unsigned int packets;

    controller();
    for (i=0;i<100;i++)
    {
        checkwriteether();
    }
}
```

C

Shared Protocol Startup

The following controller() function outlines the startup code for a shared protocol implementation. As can be seen, the baseline code follows with all other code presented in this book except for the _ACC and _DES buffer characteristic fields. In this case, the _ACC registers 0x0660 as a shared protocol with a destination address of AA-00-04-00-80-07.

```c
void controller()
{
    char device[5][6] = {"XEA0:", "XQA0:", "ESA0:", "ETA0:", "*"};
    int i, stat;

    struct
    {
        short   BFN;
        long    BFN_VAL;
        short   PTY;
        long    PTY_VAL;
        short   BUS;
        long    BUS_VAL;
        short   PAD;
        long    PAD_VAL;
        short   PRM;
        long    PRM_VAL;
        short   ETH;
        long    ETH_VAL;
        short   MLT;
        long    MLT_VAL;
        short   SHR;
        long    SHR_VAL;
        short   DES;
        short   DES_LEN;
        short   DESTYPE;
        char    a1;
        char    a2;
        char    a3;
```

```c
    char    a4;
    char    a5;
    char    a6;
} StartupBuffer =
    {
                            /* Number of receive buffers       */
    NMA$C_PCLI_BFN, 2,
                            /* Protocol                         */
    NMA$C_PCLI_PTY, 0x0660,
                            /* Size of receive buffers          */
    NMA$C_PCLI_BUS, 1500,
                            /* Padding off                      */
    NMA$C_PCLI_PAD, NMA$C_STATE_OFF,
                            /* Promiscuous mode off             */
    NMA$C_PCLI_PRM, NMA$C_STATE_OFF,
                            /* Ethernet frame format            */
    NMA$C_PCLI_FMT, NMA$C_LINFM_ETH,
                            /* Multicast mode off               */
    NMA$C_PCLI_MLT, NMA$C_PCLI_OFF,
                            /* Limited protocol access          */
    NMA$C_PCLI_ACC, NMA$C_PCLI_LIM,
                            /* Destination address              */
    NMA$C_PCLI_DES, 8, NMA$C_LINMC_SET,
        0xaa,0x00,0x04,0x00,0x80,0x07

    };

struct
    {
    int size;
    int addr;
```

```c
} StartupBufferDesscriptor =
        {
        sizeof(StartupBuffer), &StartupBuffer
        };

struct dsc$descriptor_s devicedescriptor = { 0, DSC$K_DTYPE_T, DSC$K_CLASS_S, 0};

for (i=0, stat = 0; (stat != 1) && (dev[i][0] != '*') ; i++)
{
        devicedescriptor.dsc$a_pointer = device[i];
        devicedescriptor.dsc$w_length = strlen(device[i]);
        status = sys$assign(&devicedescriptor, &channel, 0, 0);
}

if (!(status & 1)) lib$stop(status);
printf("Using ethernet controller %s\n",device[i-1]);

status = sys$qiow(0, channel, IO$_SETMODE + IO$M_STARTUP + IO$M_CTRL,iosb, 0, 0, 0,
        &StartupBufferDescriptor, 0, 0, 0, 0);

if (!(status & 1)) lib$stop(status);
if ((iosb[0] & 1) != 1)
{
        printf("ERROR : %d %d %d %d\n",iosb[0], iosb[1], iosb[2], iosb[3]);
        exit(iosb[0]);
}

}
```

Bibliography

Andrews, Gregory R. *Concurrent Programming: Principles and Practice*, Benjamin/Cummings Publishing Company, Inc., 1991.

DECNet Digital Network Architecture Phase IV: NSP Functional Specification, Digital Equipment Corporation, December 1983. AA-X439A-TK.

Goldenberg, Ruth E., and Lawrence J. Kenah. *VAX/VMS Internals and Data Structures*, Digital Press, 1991. EY-C171E-DP.

Guide to DECNet—VAX Networking, Digital Equipment Corporation, April 1988. AA-LA47A-TE.

Introduction to VMS System Services, Digital Equipment Corporation, April 1988. AA-LA68A-TE.

Martin, James, and Joe Leben. *DECNet Phase V: An OSI Implementation*, Digital Press, 1992. EY- H882E-DP.

Miller, David D., *Vax / VMS Operating Systems Concepts*, Digital Press, 1992. EY-F590E-DP

VMS I/O User's Reference Manual: Part I, Digital Equipment Corporation, June 1990. AA-LA84B- TE.

VMS I/O User's Reference Manual: Part II, Digital Equipment Corporation, April 1988. AA-LA85B- TE.

VMS Networking Manual, Digital Equipment Corporation, April 1988. AA-LA48A-TE.

VMS System Services Reference Manual, Digital Equipment Corporation, April 1988. AA-LA69A- TE.

Index

www.ingramcontent.com/pod-product-compliance
Lightning Source LLC
Chambersburg PA
CBHW051046050326
40690CB00006B/613